POSt roaD

Post Road publishes twice yearly and accepts unsolicited poetry, fiction, and nonfiction submissions. Complete submission guidelines are available at www.postroadmag.com.

Subscriptions: Individuals, $18/year; Institutions, $34/year; outside the U.S. please add $6/year for postage.

Post Road is a nonprofit 501(c)(3) corporation published by Post Road Magazine, Inc. in partnership with the Boston College Department of English. All donations are tax-deductible.

Distributed by:

Ingram Periodicals, Inc., LaVergne, TN

Printed by:

BookMasters, Mansfield, OH

Post Road was founded in New York City in 1999 by Jaime Clarke and David Ryan with the following core editors: Rebecca Boyd, Susan Breen, Hillary Chute, Mark Conway, Pete Hausler, Kristina Lucenko (1999-2003), Anne McCarty and Michael Rosovsky.

Editors Emeritus include Sean Burke (1999-2001), Jaime Clarke (1999-2008), Mary Cotton, as Publisher and Managing Editor (2004-2008), Erin Falkevitz (2005-2006), Alden Jones (2002-2005), Fiona Maazel (2001-2002), Marcus McGraw (2003-2004), Catherine Parnell, as Managing Editor (2003), Samantha Pitchel (2006-2008), and Ricco Villanueva Siasoco, as Managing Editor (2009-2010).

Cover Art:

Luis Coig, "Raw reality" (2003)

POST ROAD

Publisher
Post Road Magazine, Inc.
in partnership with the
Boston College Department
of English

Art Editor
Susan Breen

Criticism Editor
Hillary Chute

Fiction Editors
Rebecca Boyd
Mary Cotton
Michael Rosovsky
David Ryan

Guest Editor
Paul Mariani

Nonfiction Editors
Josephine Bergin
Pete Hausler
Oona Patrick

Poetry Editors
Mark Conway
Anne McCarty
Nicolette Nicola
Jeffrey Shotts
Lissa Warren

Recommendations Editors
Tim Huggins
Devon Sprague
Eugenio Volpe

Theatre Editor
David Ryan

Layout and Design
Josephine Bergin

Web Designer
David Prior

Managing Editor
Christopher Boucher

Assistant Managing Editors
Sarah Berry
Lucas Dietrich
Kacy Walz

Copyeditor
Valerie Duff-Strautmann

Interns
Trey Brewer
Kelly Cupo
Kate Iannarone
Meghan Keefe
Katherine Kim
Ana Lopez
James Melia
Geoff Pierret

Readers
Caroline Beimford
Jen Bergmark
Trey Brewer
Emily Copeland
Deirdre Costello
Kathy Douglas
Catherine Gellene
Jeff Gutierrez
Hannah Pfeifle Harlow
Kate Iannarone
Sean Keck
Meghan Keefe
Katherine Kim
Katie Kollef
Erica Plouffe Lazure
Ana Lopez
Sam Lovett
Amy Marcott
James Melia
Courtney Micksch
Brooke Olaussen
Danica Pantic
Geoff Pierret
Colette Sartor
Caitlin Seccombe
Kate Shannon
Laura Smith
Chris Staudinger
Katie Sticca
Lindsey Warren
Cedar Warman

Table of Contents

Recommendations

Guest Folio

Contributor Notes

Pearl Abraham is the author of, most recently, *American Taliban*. Her other novels are *The Seventh Beggar, Giving Up America* and *The Romance Reader*. She is also the editor of *Een Sterke Vrou: Jewish Heroines in Literature*. Her short stories and essays have appeared in various publications. "Hasidic Noir" won the 2005 Shamus award for best short story about a private eye. *The Seventh Beggar* was one of three finalists for the 2006 Koret International Award for Fiction. Abraham teaches literature and Creative Writing at Western New England College. She lives in NYC, Springfield, MA, and Columbia County, NY.

Jeffrey Alfier is a 2009 Pushcart prize nominee. His poems have appeared in *The Cape Rock*, and *Permafrost*, with work forthcoming in *Chiron Review*. His chapbooks are *Strangers Within the Gate* (2005) and *Offloading the Wounded* (2010), and he serves as co-editor of *San Pedro River Review* (www.sprreview.com).

Hannah Armbrust is a senior theatre and English major with a writing concentration at Gordon College. She is fascinated by the correlation between words and images.

Matt Bell is the author of *How They Were Found*, published by Keyhole Press in October 2010. His fiction has been included in *Best American Mystery Stories 2010* and *Best American Fantasy 2*. He is also the editor of *The Collagist* and can be found online at www.mdbell.com.

Joseph Bottum is the editor of *First Things*, one of the nation's most influential and largest-circulation monthly intellectual journals, and a contributing editor for the *Weekly Standard*. A native of South Dakota, Bottum is a graduate of Georgetown University, with a PhD in philosophy from Boston College. His essays, reviews, and poems have appeared in the *Atlantic*, the *Wall Street Journal*, the *Washington Post, Commentary, National Review*, and many other newspapers and magazines.

Jesse Cataldo lives in Brooklyn. His work has appeared in *Washington Square, Pear Noir* and *Font*.

Rebecca Chace is the author of the novel, *Leaving Rock Harbor* (Scribner, June, 2010) an "Editor's Choice" in the *New York Times Book Review*; the memoir, *Chautauqua Summer* which was a New York Times "Notable Book", as well as "Editor's Choice". She is also the author of the novel, *Capture the Flag*, which she adapted into an award winning short film with director, Lisanne Skyler. Her essay, "Looking for Robinson Crusoe" (*Fiction Magazine*) was nominated for a Pushcart prize. She can be found online at www.rebeccachace.com

Katherine Lien Chariott has published fiction and nonfiction in literary magazines including *The Literary Review, Sonora Review, upstreet* and *Columbia: A Journal of Literature and Art*. Her work can be found online in *Night Train, Kartika Review* and *Compass Rose*. She lives in Shanghai.

Emma Cline's work has appeared in *Tin House*. In 2009, she was the recipient of a Bread Loaf Writer's Conference scholarship.

Luis Coig was born in Spain, lived his teenage years in Ecuador, and moved to the United States at the age of eighteen. He earned his Masters in 1996 and had a studio in Manhattan for ten years. Now he works in a tiny home-studio in Brooklyn. To see more of Luis' artwork, visit his website at www.coig.net/luis, or his blog—currently in stasis—at http://corpuscallosum-luis.blogspot.com.

Natalie Danford is the author of a novel, *Inheritance*, and a translator and critic.

Adam Day's chapbook, "Badger, Apocrypha", won a 2010 Poetry Society of America National Chapbook Fellowship. His work has appeared in the *Boston Review*, *American Poetry Review*, *Guernica*, *The Kenyon Review*, *FIELD*, *Verse Daily*, *The Iowa Review*, *BOMB*, and elsewhere, and has been nominated for 2008 and 2009 Pushcart prizes, and included in *Best New Poets 2008*. He is the recipient of a Kentucky Arts Council grant, and a Ragdale Foundation residency He coordinates The Baltic Writing Residency in Latvia, and is a contributing editor to the online literary journal *Memorious*.

Will Dowd is an MFA student at New York University with a Master of Science from MIT. His work has appeared in *32 Poems*, *The Comstock Review*, and *Flatmancrooked's Slim Volume of Contemporary Poetry*.

Whitney Dubie lives in Burlington, VT and goes to school at Gordon College in Wenham, MA. She is studying English Language and Literature and runs cross country. She hopes to join the Peace Corps after she graduates and teach English overseas in the future. Her favorite poet and source of inspiration is Walt Whitman.

Adam Fitzgerald is a founding editor of *Maggy*. He also edits poetry for *Thumbnail Magazine*. He lives in the East Village.

Max Grinnell is a writer and college lecturer who divides his time between Boston and Chicago. He has written three books, and is currently working on a manuscript about the legacy of the Federal Writers Project's travel guides from the 1930 and 1940s. His writings can be found at www.theurbanologist.com/, and he is always up for a new adventure, with or without the promise of treasure.

A.M. Juster's fourth book, a translation of Tibullus' elegies, should be released by Oxford University Press in late 2011. His work has appeared in *The Paris Review*, *Southwest Review*, *The New Criterion*, *North American Review*, *Light* and many other publications.

Megan Kaminski is the author of two poetry chapbooks: *Across Soft Ruins* (Scantily Clad Press, 2009) and *The Prairie Opens Wide* (La Ginestra, forthcoming). Her writing has been nominated for a Pushcart prize and has been published or is forthcoming in *CutBank*, *Denver Quarterly*, *The Laurel Review*, *Phoebe*, *Third Coast*, and other fine journals. She lives in Lawrence, KS, where she teaches creative writing at the University of Kansas.

Simone Kearney has just received her MFA in poetry from Hunter College. Her most recent publications can be found in *Elimae*, *Supermachine*, *Maggy* and *Sal Mimeo*. She has worked as an assistant for poets Mark Strand and Grace Schulman, and as an intern for the Swiss artist Olaf Breuning. She is currently working at the Thierry-Goldberg Gallery on the Lower East Side. She is also a visual artist (www.simonekearney.com), and her paintings will be shown at the Morris gallery in West Cork, Ireland, this coming summer. She currently lives in Brooklyn.

Stuart Krimko is the author of *The Sweetness of Herbert* (2009) and *Not That Light* (2003), both published by Sand Paper Press in Key West, Florida. He is currently translating *Daughters of Hegel*, a 1982 novella by the Argentinian writer Osvaldo Lamborghini, into English. Krimko lives in Los Angeles, where he is an Associate Director at David Kordansky Gallery.

Award-winning author of *Dear Dante, Anxious Love*, and other works of fiction, **A. S. Maulucci** is a also a playwright, poet, and painter. His play, "Fugue for a Man and a Woman," has been staged in the US and Canada, and was performed on Connecticut Public Radio with Academy Award-winning actress, Frances McDormand. He is currently at work on a book of essays about writing. For more information, visit www.anthonymaulucci.com.

Eric Morris works as a poetry editor for *Barn Owl Review* and the Akron Series in Poetry, and his work has appeared or is forthcoming in *La Fovea, Redactions, Slant, Anti-*, and other journals. He lives and writes in Akron, Ohio, where he tries (in vain) to find a way to lift the curse of Cleveland Sports.

Angela Alaimo O'Donnell teaches English, Creative Writing, and American Catholic Studies at Fordham University in New York City. She also serves as Associate Director of Fordham's Curran Center for American Catholic Studies. Her publications include a recent collection of poems, *Moving House* (Word Press, 2009), and chapbooks *Mine* (Finishing Line Press, 2007) and *Waiting for Ecstasy* (Franciscan University, 2009). In 2011, Word Press will publish her second full-length collection, *Saint Sinatra*.

Robert Pack teaches in the Honors College at the University of Montana. His most recent book of poems is *Still Here, Still Now*, and a new collection, *Laughter Before Sleep* will be published, also by The University of Chicago Press, in 2011.

Dan Pope is the author of a novel *In The Cherry Tree* (Picador, 2003), and short stories that have been published in *Post Road, Harvard Review, McSweeney's, Iowa Review, Shenandoah, Crazyhorse*, and other literary journals. He is a graduate of the Iowa Writers Workshop and currently a writer in residence in the MFA program at Western Connecticut State University.

Allison Power is an editor for Rizzoli International Publications and edits the poetry journal *Maggy*. Her chapbook, *You Americans*, was published by Green Zone Editions in 2008. Her poems have appeared in *Pax Americana*, The Best American Poetry Blog, and *Painted Bride Quarterly*, among others. She is an MFA candidate in poetry at the New School.

Sumanth Prabhaker is the founding editor of Madras Press, a non-profit publisher of individually bound short stories and novella-length booklets that donates all net proceeds to charitable organizations selected by the authors. His novella, *A Mere Pittance*, was among the inaugural titles, and benefited Helping Hands, a program where capuchin monkeys are trained to become live-in helpers to people with physical disabilities.

Joanna Smith Rakoff's novel *A Fortunate Age* (Scribner, 2009) was awarded the Goldberg Prize for Jewish Fiction. She writes regularly for *The New York Times*, the *Los Angeles Times*, and many other publications.

Hannah Retzkin recently graduated Colorado State University with a Bachelor's in English focusing on creative writing. This is her first publication in a literary journal. She hopes to teach ESL classes abroad and travel to every continent by age thirty.

Joseph Scapellato was born in the suburbs of Chicago and earned his MFA in Fiction at New Mexico State University. Currently he teaches as an adjunct professor in the English/Creative Writing departments at Susquehanna University and Bucknell University. His work appears/is forthcoming in *The Collagist*, *SmokeLong Quarterly*, *UNSAID*, *Gulf Coast*, and others. He occasionally blogs at http://www.josephscapellato.blogspot.com/

Amy Scheibe is the author of the novel *What do You Do All Day* and writes/edits/ghostwrites/tells people what to read from her outpost in Manhattan.

Alanna Schubach's stories have appeared in *Lumina*, the *Bellevue Literary Review*, and *Underwater New York*. She lives in Fukuoka, Japan.

Jonathan Starke has essays published or appearing in *Brevity*, *Fourth Genre*, *Michigan Quarterly Review*, *The Missouri Review*, *The Normal School*, and *The Pinch*. He's also the co-founder and editor of an underdog literary journal called *Palooka*. He's currently working toward his MFA in creative writing at Colorado State University.

Bianca Stone received her MFA from NYU's creative writing program in poetry in 2009. She is the creator and co-curator of the *Ladder Poetry Reading Series* in New York City and is a regular contributor to *The The Poetry Blog*. Her most recent poetry publications include *The Patterson Literary Review*, *Fou*, *Agriculture Reader*, and *Conduit*. She is also a recent finalist for the 2010 *Crazyhorse* prize in poetry. Besides writing poetry, Bianca is also a freelance illustrator, often combining poetry and illustration. Her blog is called *Poetry Comics* (http://whoisthatsupposedtobe.blogspot.com/). She lives in Brooklyn.

Tryfon Tolides was born in Korifi Voiou, Greece. His first book, *An Almost Pure Empty Walking*, was a 2005 National Poetry Series Selection and published by Penguin in 2006. In 2009, he received a Lannan Foundation Residency in Marfa, Texas.

Christopher Tozier happily lives deep in the sand pine scrub between Paisley and Cassia, Florida. His poems have appeared in journals such as *Tampa Review*, *The Yalobusha Review*, *Saw Palm*, *The Literary Review*, *Cream City Review*, *The Florida Review*, *Maryland Poetry Review*, and *The Wisconsin Review*. He graduated from the University of Wisconsin-Madison Creative Writing and English program.

Laura van den Berg is the author of the story collection *What the World Will Look Like When All the Water Leaves Us* (Dzanc Books, 2009), which was selected for the Barnes & Noble "Discover Great New Writers" Program and shortlisted for the Frank O'Connor Award. She is the recipient of scholarships from the Bread Loaf and Sewanee Writers' Conferences, the Julia Peterkin Award, the 2009-2010 Emerging Writer Lectureship at Gettysburg College, and the 2010-2011 Tickner Fellowship at the Gilman School. She currently lives in Baltimore.

Lindsay Waters, Executive Editor for the Humanities at Harvard University Press, originated the Theory & History of Literature series at the University of Minnesota Press. At Harvard he has published, among other books, Walter Benjamin's *Selected Writings* and *The Arcades Project*, Hardt and Negri's *Empire* and *Commonwealth*, Greil Marcus's *Lipstick Traces*, and the Greil Marcus/Werner Sollors *New Literary History of America*. He has written extensively on aesthetics and is working on a book called *Slow Reading*. He published *Enemies of Promise: Publishing, Perishing, and the Eclipse of Scholarship* in 2004, and it has appeared in Portuguese, French, and Polish, and will appear in Chinese this year.

Golden State

Emma Cline

If there was a landscape that was more blessed, none of us knew it. We grew up with the sun generous and round in a blue sky, with fields and fields of dry grass. We knew from childhood the lines of the coast angled against the vast and shifting Pacific, the arc and swell, the rocky cliffs. We learned how the cows moved in the evenings, the way the creeks ran like veins across the hills, how the vast and startling sunsets appeared, biblical in their breadth and scope. We felt subtle changes of weather, the disruptions of patterns and habits, and studied the quail that made their daily migration to the oak trees behind our houses where they settled in low for the night, squawking and chittering to each other in the growing darkness.

There were the long days of waiting. We met each other in the dim sparking hours between sunset and dawn, the long night. We drove the back roads early in the morning, lights on at the convenience stores, past the shadowed oaks and houses of our sleeping families. Our parents knew how much time we spent together, at first anyways, were pleased to see us pile into packed cars, knew about the late-night drives and the parties at the wooden house outside town. They didn't know that no one lived in the wooden house, that no one owned it at all, that it was full of a strange detritus, aluminum plates and brocade armchairs, colored light bulbs and the drugs of someone long gone. We babbled incoherently, talking thickly to the speed freaks that pedaled there furiously on their lavender girls' bicycles, felt the motions of a thousand flies buzzing overhead, the floodwaters sloshing in our hearts.

It used to be that we only went there on Friday nights, left the rest of the weekend for the daytime, for the hikes with our fathers and naps on our broad leather couches. Soon we started sleeping our strange hours, waking startled and blinking in the evening light. We were groggy and distant at the dinner parties our parents gave for the conductors and art critics from the city—the circling trays of food, the drunken wives shivering alone on our balconies, gardenias drifting in the blue light of the pool. Soon enough we left that behind too, sneaking out every night to gather around the fire in back of the old house. The older boys showed us how to handle metallic powders with our bare hands while others of us diligently crushed black seeds in the corner for a foul-smelling brew.

And when deep night comes, we found beds, clustered into a close wood room, using towels for blankets. The air was heavy and still. Someone vomited silently into their cupped hands. The boys made the wet low sounds of the very drunk, the cough and hack, the moist screw in the throat. Some grabbed the hands of sleeping girls and moved them over their crotches. One muttered in his sleep, *And the dead, the dead*, while the rest of us were dreaming too; our favorite English teacher getting ripped apart by dogs in a snowstorm, stinking red tides loosed over our town, gangs of thieves roaming bleached African deserts with nowhere for us to hide.

In the small rooms the menace gathered and hung. We knew it would come, just not which night, and so, when one of the younger boys, with blood running down his face and his swollen tongue lolling, jumped head first out the attic window, it felt as though things had reached the point we had been building towards all this time, all the drugs, all the darkness, all the sly feels and ways of giving away parts of ourselves. We scattered, one of us calling the cops, the rest of us back in the cool, unfamiliar sheets of our bedrooms, twitching wildly with nervous energy. For days we saw black snakes sudden and stark in our path, lizards scattering, a coyote waiting under the stairs. There was danger everywhere. Always the shadowed figure of the stranger cutting across an empty, moonlit field.

The city razed the wooden house, while our parents asked us if we had known the boy. We said, of course, that we hadn't, and it was true. They would ask us this many times again, because this guy was just the first in a long line. We got to an age where people we know started to die. It happened around high school graduation; the first mention in the newspaper of a boy crashing his truck at three in the morning, along the string of 101. The freshman who killed himself with his father's shotgun in his basement the week before homecoming, the girl from high school who drowned in the Russian River. Your first kiss, your choir teacher's daughter, the vice-president of the junior class. The deaths stacked up. And they were written about in the dulcet, innocuous tones of our small-town newspapers, the sports, the hobbies, the dental-hygienist dreams. The radio played Teen Angel on a loop that summer, while the local DJ jokingly kept a death watch, promising a case of Coca Cola to the family of the teen with the prettiest yearbook photo;

Just sweet sixteen, and now you're gone
They've taken you away.
Are you somewhere up above
And I am still your own true love
I'll never kiss your lips again
They buried you today

We all knew about the time the dead girl took off her shirt and bared her breasts to a crowd, danced languidly in a darkened room, but we kept it quiet, drank a beer to her memory.

Everyone was scared then, felt the fear of our parents in waves. We rolled away from each other like marbles, some of us to the junior college, some of us staying home. None of us encountered anything but aimlessness, dreamy days that turned lazily around and around. Our parents had expectations but let us easily shrug them off, pleased when we shaved, went walking, groomed our horses or idly baked zucchini bread from the harvest of our mothers' gardens. What they couldn't know was how far away we were by then, how much things seemed to have shifted. We couldn't stop our minds from catching again and again on the fact of the bodies, the splintered bones and leaking hearts. We dreamt endlessly of a meeting between the dead in an empty ballroom, watched the town erect a huge white cross strung with lights on the hillside above the football field. Though we made our movements away from each other, lived alone in apartments, and held jobs, bought groceries and pickup trucks, we never forgot those sparks at the back of our throats, the dark pale sky of early morning.

The first night we were together again, we drank sweet wine in the high hills of someone's parent's vineyard, in a row of vines. The summer wind rose, a dry heavy heat, and we lay back and took off our clothes, all of us, our white limbs clustered together in the moonlight. Later we rode our bicycles down the rows of vines, following the dark roads of the ranch to the meadow to feel the horses' brambly breathing against our bare chests. We rubbed the foamy sweat that secretes itself in their curves across our arms, touched it to our necks to feel the moist heat of it. Some of us walked silently into the pond, floating on our backs where the daylight warmth collects, diving down to the muddy depths, letting the black water rise up and catch our hair. We gasped for breath, while the harvest moon kept the rest of us dazed and circling the banks.

It was like the old times, but better. We spent the hours gathering what we needed: the wet stones from the lake's edge, the turkey feathers with their calcified hollows. The chimney swifts swooped low over us, heading south. We made piles of leaves arranged by shape, by minute changes of color, found soft-skinned Chanterelles burning under a stutter of leaves, carried them like babies in our arms. We crushed silt-red rocks for a dry pigment we mixed with water and marked our bodies with, concentric circles around our stomach, rings up our legs, streaks drying stiff and tight under our eyes. We flaked off the crust to feel it sting.

Our wealthy parents—the San Francisco high-society philanthropists, old sitcom actresses holed up in sprawling estates in Healdsburg—didn't mind us living on the rocky part of Sonoma Mountain where grapes were hard to grow. We mapped the land, roving with our picnics and the old simple guitars. The girls made rosemary pan–bread and black beans in coffee cans while the boys roasted peppers and corn tortillas, and it all tasted like fire. At first we camped in our parents' nylon sleeping bags, high on the grassy ridge over the lake, but soon enough, structures started to rise, rigged in trees, dug into the hillside, made of mud, sheets of cotton and car doors, corrugated tin and hay bales. They were beautiful, and the girls would make velvet curtains from their first communion dresses, and the boys kept the dirt down in the roads and offered up shirtfuls of dark berries for the girls' white bowls. We dragged together beds and hung paper lanterns in the trees, lit them as darkness came on, played volleyball under their diffuse glow. We danced in two circles, like we'd been taught as children, the give and take, hand over wrist, the dizzy, reeling turns. They trucked in an old church organ from town, and we spent the nights wine-drunk and smeared, someone playing murder ballads and the sweet religious songs from our childhoods while our voices met under the fixed and radiant stars and our hearts opened like hothouse flowers.

Reporters liked to make the things we did sound dirty, make it sound like the guys forced the girls into it. That wasn't true, not at all. There was an incense we burned sometimes that made us all drowsy, made us feverish and yielding. Girls read aloud from sacred texts and back issues of *Playboy*, one hand on the page and the other hand unbuttoning their blouse, five shameless mouths on you at once, it didn't matter whose, Some girls tucked their long hair into caps and wrestled in the grass like men. They tricked the boys into posing for obscene and luminous polaroids they secreted away and traded like baseball cards. We felt so generous with one another, someone's finger in your mouth making you tremble like a bass string, warm breasts in your hands like full-bellied birds.

We used an embroidery needle and India ink, tattooing blue ships in full sail on each other's backs, interlocking hearts on the white expanse of our thighs. These were the symbols we recognized each other by, the striated feathers that came to us in dreams, the silhouettes of Western mountain ranges, religious medals we had won in some other life.

And when October came, and the girls among us grew swollen and tight in the belly, it was better. It was life, at least, fecundity, none of the death or darkness that riddled that old wooden house, that left us dead too. We imagined growing corn in the high heat of summer and canning peaches for the winter, drying sheets of lemon verbena under the noonday sun, jam bubbling hot and dark in cast-iron pots. We would all be their parents, since no one would know whose child was whose, and the children would know about moss, about snake skins and maps, and they would pick apart owl pellets to birth the bones of mice beneath their hands.

And so it came to be, the main house, the babies born, all of us growing together into women and men. Our hen-house was papered with pages from *Rolling Stone* and our children charted the voyage of the planets in the dirt with their fingers, rode together to the pond on the back of their Indian pony. We trusted the magnetics, our ripe-red hearts, the hills that take human shape and remind us who we are. ❧

NOON

NOON

A LITERARY ANNUAL

1324 LEXINGTON AVENUE   PMB 298   NEW YORK   NEW YORK   10128

EDITION PRICE $9 DOMESTIC $14 FOREIGN

Olive Higgins Prouty's NOW, VOYAGER

Joanna Smith Rakoff

These days, when Olive Higgins Prouty's name is mentioned, it's generally in passing reference to Sylvia Plath, who, as rabid Plath fans know, attended Smith College on a scholarship funded by Prouty and got to know the lady writer rather well, through a written correspondence and an equally quaint series of teas in the drawing room of Prouty's well-appointed Brookline manse. As it turned out, benefactor and beneficiary were eerily well-matched: like Plath, Prouty suffered from depression. At twelve, she'd had her first breakdown. A second followed, in 1925, when Prouty was in her early forties, a few years after the death of her one-year-old daughter, Olivia. A quarter-century later, when Plath took a handful of sleeping pills and crawled under her childhood home, it was Prouty who oversaw her recovery, arranging and paying for her stay at McLean and offering comfort and guidance to Plath and her family. And ten-odd years after *that*, Plath would caricature Prouty in *The Bell Jar* as Philomena Guinea, a fusty, outmoded novelist—pathetically unaware of her own bourgeois limitations—who plays the same role in the life of Plath's heroine, Esther Greenwood, as did Prouty in Plath's own life, ushering her to a posh mental institution and suchlike.

If Plath's characterization was perhaps a bit too severe—particularly considering the generosity Prouty had shown her—it wasn't, at least superficially, all that off-base: by 1963, the year of Plath's second, successful suicide attempt—and the British release of *The Bell Jar*—Prouty's literary and popular reputation had declined so dramatically that her novels, to a one, had fallen out of print and she couldn't find a publisher for her memoirs. Prouty's style and ostensible subject matter—the social constraints placed on young women of privilege—had largely fallen out of fashion. Literate youngsters like Plath were not reading *Stella Dallas*, Prouty's 1925 bestseller, an account of maternal devotion that, in comparison with the groundbreaking novels of the day, seemed mawkish and sentimental, its values reminiscent of the Victorian era of Prouty's birth. No, they were reading *On the Road* and *Goodbye, Columbus*, *Rabbit, Run*, and *Henderson the Rain King*, or, in the more popular vein, Rona Jaffe's *The Best of Everything*, say, which chronicled with heartbreaking precision the first wave of women to enter the white-collar workforce in large numbers, as secretaries in the 1950s, and the difficulties these women faced, torn between domestic life—the pressure to have a family—and the novel pleasures of independence, not to mention intellectual fulfillment.

As it happens, these are precisely the themes that define Prouty's novels, proto-feminist parables about bright young women who don't, for various reasons, find themselves able to follow the grain of mainstream society. That such novels registered with the reading public of interwar America is hardly surprising—gender roles were rapidly changing in the 1920s and 30s, paving the way for the vast upheavals that Jaffe chronicled in 1959—and, despite Plath's assessment, Prouty's novels did indeed find wide audiences. In 1950, when the two writers first made their acquaintance, Prouty's best-known novel, *Now, Voyager*—released in 1941 and followed by a film adaptation with Bette Davis in 1942—was still on bookshelves of every middle class home in the country. An immediate sensation, *Now, Voyager* alights with Charlotte Vale, a wealthy and well-born Bostonite of a certain age, as she tours the Mediterranean on an ocean liner, her trunk filled with the clothing of her sister-in-law, Lisa. Slowly, Prouty reveals that this cruise represents a sort of therapy for Charlotte who, months earlier, had suffered a nervous collapse, precipitated by years of even greater suffering under the hand of her tyrannical mother, who had kept Charlotte, the child of her old age, chained to her side. Once freed from Mother Vale, Charlotte had lost twenty-five pounds, chopped off her Victorian mound of hair, and generally reinvented herself as a modern woman, with the help of an Austen Riggs-style psychiatrist and the clear-headed Lisa.

Often described as a romance, *Now, Voyager* is anything but, despite the fact that Charlotte does indeed fall in love—a doomed sort of love—with a married man she meets on board the ship. Prouty renders their affair, tentative and fumbling at first, in some semblance of real time, making vivid the excruciating terror, confusion, and exhilaration that accompanies real—rather than sentimental—romance. When J.D. first kisses Charlotte—who has gone more than thirty years with only a kiss or two—she wonders, with gorgeous realism, if she responds "from her own desire, or submission to his." Who hasn't, on some level, felt this way?

Eventually it becomes clear that Charlotte's desire is very much in evidence—though Prouty, true to the mores of her day, omits the tawdry details in favor of limning her heroine's psyche—and though they part ways, knowing they have no future together, this taste of love, of erotic fulfillment, is enough to allow Charlotte to return to Boston and stand up to her mother. What transpires there, you'll have to read the novel to discover.

And certainly you should. Prouty is not—I'm not going to pretend otherwise—by any means a great novelist—her over-use of exclamation points alone is enough to set one's teeth on edge—but she is a rather good one, and she's certainly a far cry from Philomena Guinea. There's a further irony to Plath's parody of her, by the way, which you may have already guessed: *Now, Voyager*'s tremendous success had to do, in part, with Prouty's unabashedly honest depiction of Charlotte's nervous breakdown and subsequent hospitalization. In 1941 the concept of psychiatric treatment was still shocking in and of itself, and the novel found thousands of readers purely on the basis of the glimpse it provided into a mental institution. By today's standards, of course, Prouty's account is pretty tame— no straightjackets, no electroshock therapy, no catatonics moaning in corners—but today's standards were, of course, established by none other than *The Bell Jar.* ๛

Rebuilding Aesthetics from the Ground Up

Lindsay Waters

"I've got a twelve-year old son, and he's always bored, and so am I."
—*Thelonius Monster (aka Bob Forrest)*

"Irony and ridicule are entertaining and effective, and. . . at the same time
they are agents of a great despair and stasis in U.S. culture. . ."
—*David Foster Wallace*

I am concerned about my ability to feel things. Artworks are contraptions manufactured and designed to trigger feeling. So many now claim they have difficulty feeling art—so many, I had not thought anomie had undone so many. Didn't Dr. Johnson say that "when people tire of Beijing, they have become tired of living"? So what is going on? Many of us appear to have grown to be anaesthetized to life. One main idea running through elite discourse in the 20th century in Europe shortly after E.M. Forster announced his mantra to the world, "Only Connect," was the rise of the fashion for disconnecting things, everything. Atomism, incommensurability, was the rule from Bertrand Russell in the first decades of the century to Paul de Man when we reached the last decades. Holism was trashed for being so 19th century!

We are suffering from a shortage of feelings. And it's not just Wall Street bankers, but even noted American novelists like Don DeLillo who seem to be stuck in the doldrums, revealing, as the *New York Review of Books* puts it, only a sort of "studied numbness" that seems to be designed to convey "existential bafflement and dismay."

Where and how exactly do we start to reverse direction so we can begin to create the links to build a future? If there is to be an anthropology of the future, humans have to be inserted back into the whole equation, and the equation has to have some ability to give a total explanation. We airbrushed humans out of the picture in the 20th century. Airbrushing them out was the nicest thing we did to them in that time period. As you remember, we were massively successful killing them, maiming them, and burning them up in heaps like the underbrush of the forest that needs to be removed. What is the nature of this process of eliminating humans on the intellectual level or of emptying them out? How might it be reversed? What does it really look and feel like, this aesthetic lassitude?

We live in a time not of elation, but dejection. Human emotional history as it works for groups goes in waves that carry thousands, if not millions, in their tides. Humans were "up" during the Renaissance in Europe, during the Romantic period, and during the 60s. All you have to do is read a bit of Renaissance literature to get the sense that many people then were feeling up about themselves and the world. We are down now, many of us (which is not to deny that there are always lots of us working at cross purposes with the times).

One form our negativism takes is the resistance to art. What is the contemporary history of the resistance to art and to the feelings art provokes? I now have a sense of awakening aesthetic enjoyment, but just a few years ago I strongly resisted engagement with new art. Before it was as if all the feelings with which I might have engaged art—the bright colors, the rousing rhythms, the upbeats—were cauterized. If medical treatment is not an option and supplies are unavailable, sometimes cauterizing the wound is the best option. You take a fire-heated piece of metal to cauterize a wound in order to stop the bleeding and close it. Cauterizing a wound is a dangerous and painful way to treat an injury. In some extreme cases, however, it might be the best option.

When I was very young, my feelings were cauterized. I was raised in a Roman Catholic community, one that was largely Irish Catholic, but Belgian as well. Everyone knows about the priests who abused little boys, but I had kept my distance from the priests by not becoming an altar boy. My desensitization had nothing to do with suspecting them, and everything to do with my general negativism and also with the fatalism that is so dominant in that culture. Many have a sense of this life from reading the Irish writers, James Joyce first of all, and then Flann O'Brien and John McGahern. When I first read Joyce's *Portrait*, I thought it was an autobiography—mine. More recently I had that story re-inscribed in my flesh by reading an anthropologist's account of her two years of research into the life of a West Irish farm community. My family has been gone from those parts since the 1850s, but it was as if we still lived there in terms of what's central to my aesthetic life, the cultivation of the feelings: not really their education, but their suppression. When I read Nancy Scheper-Hughes's description of "this apparent state of lovelessness, lack of tenderness, and consequent feelings of psychological abandonment and loss" and "the basic emotional cast of the 'Irish personality,'" it all rang true, down to the last detail, to the very language of it all, words the people there in the West use now and words my mother used. This includes the idea that anyone who wants to live a different sort of life is a "traitor." I have found myself holding back, engulfed by what Durkheim calls "anomie," and motivated by a moralistic feeling that it is best to keep my family secrets hidden, because I did not want to betray my clan by telling their secrets.

When I was in second grade, the forty or fifty of us packed into the classroom had a tender, young, vulnerable nun who held us captive for many days by telling us the story of Maria Goretti. Today, you can Google Maria Goretti and find out that she lived, that her life was so sensational that movies have been made about her, and that the Catholic Church made her a saint since I first heard her life graphically recounted to me. She was murdered by age eleven. For me, for decades, her story was a lurid wound burned into my soul by a seemingly sweet, beautiful nun who had probably never been kissed, who probably lived in fear of being touched by a boy, and it made me afraid of being touched by people and art.

In those days I was terrified by the story of the big, bad wolf who disguised himself as a lamb, and for good reason: I was getting to know the truth of that fairy tale myself in St. Pat's grade school in St. Charles, Illinois. This story of sexual abuse in fact was in its telling to our group of eight-year olds an act of abuse. Did I tell my parents what happened at school those days? Of course not. Fifty little children huddled alone in that room listening to the sweet voice of the nun tell them a story so terrible they had to dig deeper inside the dark space in the closet of their mind to hide. The feeling of inchoate fury that lodged itself in my body beneath the level of cognition convinced me of one thing: don't let this happen to you. Don't be like the little nun. Stay away. Young, dimpled, and wimpled as she was, she was my Ancient Mariner whose tale of horror spooked me for life, and made my heart "as dry as dust."

I learned as a child that there were many things that were so painful that I did not want to know about them. A different way to do things would be to do what Emerson did when his son Waldo died: he faced it. He wrote about it. I suppressed my experience. I did not face it in its horror. I was shocked by what the "kind, sweet nun" told me. She told me that Maria Goretti was threatened by a neighbor boy. He wanted to have sex with her. She wanted to preserve her virginity. As I remember the story, Maria carved a piece of wood into a knife and killed herself rather than have sex with the boy. What I took from the story was the lesson that sexual pleasure is bad and is to be resisted at all costs, even suicide. God would prefer I kill myself rather than have unwanted sex. The years I heard that story were the years that the line "better dead than red" were popular among rightists in America. Better the A-bomb than Communist socialism. You see how the lesson the child is told in school is connected to the biggest international, sociohistorical, geopolitical questions. There truly was no place to hide from the big historical questions, even for an 8 year-old. The nun who beat us with ping-pong paddles in third grade only seemed to be more violent. (No wonder I've always been a little reluctant to play ping-pong.)

We spent so much time in class with the nun trying to help us imagine our souls concretely as a milk bottle that could be filled with milk or emptied because of our sins. We never considered that our milk bottles could be emptied out by our parents and nuns and priests. But the culture of guilt-ridden American Irish Catholicism, whose agent this nun was, all worked to snuff our souls out by torture. Torture is used to cause the tortured person to suffer a loss of autonomy and to revert to an earlier behavioral level. [1] For an eight-year-old that means reverting to a level lower than the age of reason when one could exercise self-consciousness. It means the eradication of self-consciousness. In my life I have only recently, that is within the last ten years—to be clear that is after the age of fifty—come to a sense of my self as having a self. I am not blaming this one nun. The whole cultural system of which I was a part conspired to cause me to not develop self-consciousness of the sort most humans possess. "Regressing the subject, destroying its capacity to be complex within itself, that is the effect of torture." [2]

I will grant you that it is paradoxical that a culture that encourages the sensual enjoyment of incense, stained-glass windows, bread and wine, and song is simultaneously trying to terrify its members out of enjoying the material world. The pop star Madonna got a lot of her edge because she knew how to dance right on the knife's edge that separates the two sides of this paradox. [3] I have mentioned the paradox of puritanism in Irish Catholicism. It is also paradoxical that a society such as the U.S. that portrays itself as the leading promoter of the individual and his or her rights should be a champion promoter of conformism, guilt, and repression, but Nathaniel Hawthorne's Hester Prynne gets her edge because she also dances on the edge of that paradox. She makes salient the hypocrisy of Americans who champion the right to individual self-expression and make it virtually impossible, excruciatingly painful to exercise. No human could dare be as bold as Hester. She was a fiction.

So when the young and very improper hillbilly girl who was my babysitter turned me on to radio stations WLS and WJJD and Elvis, it's a wonder I opened up to her and them, but I did. The only force that could

---

[1] Adapted from a lecture given at the Anthropological Futures Conference, Institute of Ethnology, Academia Sinica, Taiwan, June 12-13, 2010, and a Conference organized by the editors of the journal Boundary 2 at the University of Hong Kong on June 16, 2010. I am grateful to the comments of Paul Carter, Allen Chun, Rob Wilson, Paul Bové, and Jonathan Arac. See quotation from CIA policy on torture in Paul Bové, Poetry against Torture (Hong Kong: University of Hong Kong Press, 2009), p. 134.

[2] Bové, p. 135.

[3] As Rob Wilson pointed out to me in discussion of this paper, all Catholicisms are not the same. Irish Catholicism was shaped by the divisions in Europe of the 17th century that forced men who wanted to become priests to go to France to study for the priesthood. There they absorbed a lot of what we think of as Protestant loathing of the flesh. Italian Catholicism—think of Madonna or Caravaggio—celebrates the flesh.

prevail against such an insidious force as what was unleashed on us children is a force that also works on as many levels, a full-body force: art. Music won my heart and showed there was an alternative to repression. Music has ways to overcome the censor inside us that nothing else in life does, because it is the art that is non-verbal and non-conceptual.

When we repressed our feelings, we also repressed any sense of ourselves as subjects, souls that connected the fragments of our world into wholes. We gloried in the disarray. We developed an ideal for ourselves of the person who did not and would not connect things. I admired de Man when he said in his essay "Shelley Disfigured" that no thing can be connected to any other thing, thinking it right to reverse all the shoddy linkages people had touted. But I now question what he said and see it in the context of Bertrand Russell's Logical Atomism and the willful disintegration of the world into bits in line with a brutal reductionism that became the default position of the elite in the West from the onset of World War I to the financial crisis of 2008, a willful refusal to connect the dots fueled by greed. "Bitsiness as Usual," I call it. What Benjamin called the "mimetic faculty," the ability to see analogies and use them to build connections, gave way to the slide into belief in a doctrine of incommensurability. The ability to imagine similarities and to mimic other creatures and things has been one of the highest abilities of humans, but like the ability to have experiences it has been on the wane especially in the 20th century. [4]

But some of the supposed advances of the twentieth century are being reversed. The fact/value distinction has collapsed, as Hilary Putnam argued in his 2002 book. It is time to leave the philosophies of the twentieth century behind us. This philosophical triumph of facts as they can be established by science over the messy realm of feeling is, in fact, much older than the one century. It did not begin thirty years ago with the triumph of the science and technology faculties over the humanities faculty in the wake of Heidegger-gate and de Man-gate. No, the triumph of the scientistic world view with its emphasis on logic and method over the irrationality of the arts goes back to the rise of the Royal Society in the 1680s after the disaster of the wars of religion. It is from this moment on that the emotions have been shamed into silence. It's been a dominant view for centuries.

I am really interested when people talk about renouncing selfhood as if it were some sort of great human achievement like climbing Mont Blanc. Rich people do the darndest things!! They light their cigars with hundred dollar bills because they can. In my America, we imagined that Europeans did sophisticated things like that, like glorying in the death of the subject. Well, think about this: In China, as Wang Hui shows, all those

---

[4] *Walter Benjamin, "On the Mimetic Faculty," Selected Writings, vol. 2, pp. 720-722, p. 720.*

celebrating postmodernism are pro-business Neoliberals. In America they are, too, but they don't know it, and no one has sent them the message that Bob Dylan was ridiculing those who celebrated life on Maggie's Farm. Ignorance is bliss. This was and is our poverty. This is the situation from which I believe we can rise up, not perhaps in splendor, but in dignity. We are Eliot's Prufrock, his Tiresias, and we are Benjamin's collector (as sadly described by Ackbar Abbas), the "impotent individual." We are Adam and Eve the way they look in Masaccio's fresco after they've been cast out of the garden.

We have suffered a fatal loss of the ability to absorb new historical occurrences, Walter Benjamin argued. Men and now women go off to war and come back unable to say anything coherent about what happened to them. So he said in his essay on Leskov, and he says it also in his 1933 essay "Experience and Poverty." My father went AWOL after he was assigned to do desk work in the Quartermaster's Corp in the Pacific in World War II and told to travel up to Cheyenne, Wyoming, and catch a troop train to California to join the war in progress in 1942. He went home to Denver and sat there listlessly until the Military Police came and took him away and put him on a train. By then he'd been reassigned to work on a landing craft—essentially, a death sentence. But two Purple Hearts later the war was over and he went home, and we, his nine kids, did not get a word out of him about how it had been in New Guinea and Borneo. Given a death sentence, he ended up as silent as Bartleby about what it had been like. There'd been a change in the structure of experience, Benjamin claimed; that sounds right to me. (My father was perhaps a little ahead of the game in being unable to share experiences before the war as well as after it.)

Warfare in the age of large-scale industrialism was alienating. Newspaper accounts of the war reinforced the drive to alienate humans from experience offering up tons and tons of information totally lacking in connections between the individual news items. Freud had argued that our consciousness was supposed to protect us against the bombardment of stimuli: "For a living organism, protection against stimuli is almost more important than the reception of stimuli," he wrote. Benjamin, in "On Some Motifs in Baudelaire," comments that "the threat posed by these energies [of the stimuli] is the threat of shocks." How then, asks Benjamin, can these stimuli be a fertile breeding ground for poetry? Baudelaire "made it his business to parry the shocks, no matter what the source, with his spiritual and physical self." Baudelaire noted that the exemplary writer of modern life, Constantine Guys, stood at his desk like a soldier at combat. And he believed that the shock experience of the person walking in the big city was like the "isolated 'experiences' of the worker at his machine." All these modern people have been "cheated out of" experience (196). They have been anaesthetized, and their lives and the poetry written about it, like that of Baudelaire's, "imparts a sense of boundless desolation." For "it is this very inability to experience that explains the true nature of rage" (200). Time in the modern mood of spleen is history-less because spleen "exposes the isolated experience in all its nakedness" (202). What Benjamin says corresponds with what Sianne Ngai says in her book *Ugly Feelings*. She quotes approvingly Adorno's comments on the "social ineffectuality" of the autonomous high modernist art work. She is not saying she loves this situation, but she's saying this analysis fits the modernist situation best, which is one when it is as much as we can expect of art that it conveys to us matters of "inter-est"—information, not inspiration. We have undergone, and the art we produce has undergone a change, and what has occurred, as she says, is "a certain vitiation of aesthetic experience in general." In our engagements with art now it seems as if there has come about "the extinction of a certain *specific capacity for aesthetic perception* caused by it." When Benjamin wrote his "Work of Art" essay, his friends like Adorno seemed to have thought it was their job to wrangle with him and argue him out of the views he was expressing. "'You certainly don't mean that, Wally,' said Teddy. 'You're making a grand mistake getting all tangled up in your emotions, and you have failed to deal with things properly, which is to say, conceptually. Let me tell you what you mean to say. It is exactly what I wrote in the essay I sent to you two months ago, which you have obviously been having some trouble getting to or understanding.'" They made a mistake, I think, that I am tempted to make with Ngai's work, which is to say she is wrong, because I don't like the situation she is analyzing. Benjamin's friends terrorized him and delayed publication of his work for years. I don't want to repeat their shameful performance; I want to reflect on what Ngai says, because it makes me realize the degree to which things have shifted in art-making and art-receiving. Did art lose the capacity to shock or did we lose the capacity to feel? My sense that I do have aesthetic experiences happens in a context that has been well analyzed by Baudelaire, Benjamin, and Ngai. In any case, I do not think the new indifference to art is really so new. In fact, it has a noble lineage in the West, and one that is so paradoxical it can confuse the innocent and the learned. In the parish of the West where I was brought up, as I said before, we were taught to give ourselves over to stained-glass windows and forbidden to assent to much else that gave pleasure.

If I want to argue that things can happen otherwise, as I do, it is with an understanding that it is not any longer a foregone conclusion that I or anyone else can have an aesthetic experience that bears any resemblance to the experience of the sublime that Wordsworth had crossing the Alps. No one can take it for granted that they simply experience things as an independent subject. Consciousness itself is contested. Perhaps, I would argue, it always was, even back in those centuries when people took it for granted.

The most peculiar and powerful thing for me about the Coen Brothers' movie *No Country for Old Men* is the way it continually surprises the viewer, so continually that there seems no way that seeing the movie can end being an experience for the viewer.[5] It seems to preclude ever becoming what Benjamin calls "Erfahrung." It seems to embody exactly what Benjamin theorized about the dearth of experience in modern life. Also, if you have never been pistol-whipped, and want to feel what it's like vicariously, this would be an ideal opportunity. There is a neat fit between what the central character in the movie, Sheriff Ed Tom Bell (Tommy Lee Jones) says and what Benjamin wrote about how life nowadays has changed so much that a person who is traditionally minded like the Sheriff feels like he wants to retire. Crime along the Tex/Mex border has become so different in kind from what it used to be, because of the grisly violence of criminals and the scale of their crimes, that a person like himself feels shocked every day. Not so long ago war was cavalry on horseback and swords and hand-to-hand combat; now it is large numbers of men flung together using machine guns and some in airplanes dropping bombs on people they cannot even see. Everything has speeded up. A "man has to put his soul at hazard," he says, under these new conditions. The very first thing that happens in the movie is that an unsuspecting deputy is violently strangled by the exceedingly strange-looking, indeed freaky, Anton Chigurth, who then proceeds to perform one barbaric act after another, at such a pace and all so graphically presented to the audience that Chigurth seems to be literally a new mutant form of human, a monster so cold-blooded no one, not even some other near-monsters, most notably the hired gun played by Woody Harrelson, can prepare to do combat with him. The scene is rural Texas on the border with Mexico, and the cops and citizenry seem very old-fashioned walking, talking, and driving at a slow pace, sayin everythin with a drawl, dropping all their g's.

The movie, I found, constantly surprised me because I was constantly saying to myself, "OK, this Chigurth seems to be a monster, but he is certainly not going to outwit each and every single one of the people who tries to arrest him." Stupid me. Most affecting was the way when I felt, OK, he won't be able to top what he just did in terms of brutality, he did just that. The final straw was when he killed the sweet and innocent wife of the hunter who'd chanced upon the scene of carnage that took place in a drug deal that went bad on a large scale leaving six men and two dogs

---

[5] *On the movie, I have profited from reading the entry by David Thomson in his* Have You Seen? A Personal Introduction to 1000 Films *(New York: Knopf, 2008), p. 603, and his essay on Tommy Lee Jones in* The Guardian.

dead.

The effect of the movie seems to be exactly what Benjamin says: because the surprises keep coming as if fired at you by a machine gun, you cannot take them in. The movie threatens to leave the viewer wasted, spent, numb, utterly desensitized, anaesthetized to the ongoing carnage. Everything is so homely, so downhome, but what happens is so grotesque, so uncouth, so barbaric, such an outrage to the very notion of home that the movie comes in below the radar and strafes, bombs, and rapes you. It's as if there were a rape up in Garrison Keillor's Lake Woebegone. Almost all the victims of Chigurth submit to him like lambs to slaughter, wide-eyed and naïve. Nice people are not prepared to protect themselves from the jackals at loose in the world today. Hitler was an outrage, but he was off the charts outrageous. Now we have Hitlers everywhere at the post offices and your own stock broker's office. Evil has mutated, and Hannah Arendt is a prophet. As Benjamin said, the human imagination for art and creation has not kept pace with the human imagination for violence and crime. One person says he is working hard "lookin for what's comin" and another comments "No one can see that."

Again and again the movie suggests that what it's presenting to us will go beyond our ability to assimilate it to our experience. What happens in the movie would certainly go beyond the experience of most people, but is it true that even the experience of watching the movie goes beyond what we can assimilate to our experience? Does the movie contribute to anaesthetizing us to what we might experience of it? Perhaps Benjamin is right that with the advances in movie technology a completely new poverty has descended on mankind. Does the artmaking of the Coen Brothers make for movies that anaesthetize their viewers?

I'd argue that the carefully arranged-for heightening of outrageous incidents in this movie does just the opposite of anaesthetizing. The key tool for anaesthetizing someone by torture is to batter them with a set of experiences that they cannot respond to as if they were a series. The key is to assault them with attacks that seem totally disconnected. The events in *No Country* seem to be of just that sort, but in fact they proceed—I could show—in a steady uphill progression until Carla Jean, the wife of the likeable but foolish hunter, Llewleyn Moss, gets killed. What McCarthy and the Coen Brothers do is a bit like what Shakespeare does in *King Lear*—kill all the good people off one by one making sure to kill Cordelia ignominiously, while all the worst bastards go scot free. *King Lear*, says Harold Bloom, is the most nihilistic work of literature in the Western canon. Most nihilistic and most affirmative in a bizarre way. The way the story and the movie are constructed poetically is manifest to those with eyes to see if they just stop covering them with their hands. The machinery does not clank, but it nearly does. But this is the way that the artists are preparing their audience to survive this moment in history, by showing us that the malevolent forces in our society nearly have it all under their control. The situation is nearly so bad that the only thing to do is despair the way the Sheriff is threatening to do. And yet, and yet, the movie-makers are preparing us emotionally to at least not commit suicide. If some intelligence can make this movie, perhaps there is a little bit of reason for hope. As Benjamin says, there is hope, just not for us. The movie threatens to blast and bomb our senses until we are insensate, and then it really does not do that. It has measure of a sort that the Frankenstein-like monster Chigurth, whose appetite for torturing his fellow humans knows no bounds, does not have; and that offers a small measure of relief in a world otherwise totally black. The way the movie manages light and darkness to achieve effect is worthy of the closest study. Keeping the audience alert from frame to frame as they search for what is salient is an art that many filmmakers have cast aside as too challenging to viewers used to watching the TV, and it is risky to not make it easy for the viewers, but the Coen Brothers are willing to take that risk and thereby delight some of us.

So I think we can reverse the direction we have been following toward greater and greater clamping down on feeling, but the way we get to feel again may not be exactly fun. I discovered that the forces working to squash my feelings could not exercise full dominion over me when I learned that some songs that played on my mother's radio had wormed their way into my consciousness, songs like Perry Como's "Catch a Falling Star": "Put it in your pocket, never let it fade away, for love may come and tap you on the shoulder some starless night, and just in case you think you want to hold her, you'll have a pocket full of starlight." Did I come to love the stars that shone through the trees over the No-Name Lake at Beida because of the influence of Perry Como's song? I would not be surprised. And stars are part of constellations, and constellations name a principle of linking things together poetically that militates against the atomism enforced by the eliminative materialists among the analytic philosophers. I had a notion that consciousness and soulfulness were something you had in full all your life or you did not forever. Standing up for myself, alone, and letting the world affect me: this is the transformation I am interested in encouraging. "Our souls are not given, we 'become' souls," writes Isabelle Stengers.

How does this movie get me to engage in a spiritual exercise and one that enlivens my soul? It is by throwing me back on myself. I will not find an explanation for the evil in the world in the movie. And as long as I keep lamenting with the Sheriff that we seem to have fallen as a race off the cliff and there is no continuity between now and back then when our ancestors lived, I will be looking for explanations for the situation in all the wrong places. For one thing, there is no explanation. What there might be is a transformation of my consciousness. My judgment that I like or dislike a work depends on its challenging me in a way that tests my mettle and gives me a sense of my self. This stance sounds so American, and it is, even if Americans often betray it by falling into conformism. But the stance is also not foreign to China, for it is the one embraced by Lu Xun in his 1908 essay "Po esheng lun" ("On a refutation of malevolent voices"). In this essay, according to Wang Hui, who recently performed a philological analysis of it at a conference at Harvard, Lu Xun tried to develop a new, archaic voice.[6] And he is also calling for a re-enchantment of the world so that it can be experienced with deep feeling. ❧

---

[6] *Wang Hui, Harvard lecture, 6 March 2010. I have also had the chance to read the commentary on Wang Hui's paper by Theodore Huters.*

Luis Coig: Paintings

In my work I explore the intersections between the scientific and mystical worldviews with equal amounts of contempt and respect for both. As is the case with most people, a great part of my sensitivity, my attitude toward the world, was shaped when I was a teenager. At the time, I happened to live in Ecuador, a country of colorful traditions and fabulous biodiversity that lives in my memory as an enchanted land. I became very interested in nature and the magical worldview of native peoples. Many of my pieces conjure up the impressions of this part of my life.

I derive a lot of inspiration from empirical scientific discoveries and I have a passion for biology in particular, but I also consider equally important the intuitive aspect of the human mind. The realm of the imagination is interwoven with the world of dreams and numinous visions. And true art of any kind is very much like dreams in that it reveals itself through nuance and connotation. My intention is always to create works that allow for various interpretations and hint at multiple meanings.

In 2007, I completed 102 Tiny American Paintings. Some of its constituent parts appear in this issue. This work is an investigation into the tendency of the human mind to play and how that activity drives the creative process. Using humor as my vehicle, I explore a world of folly and incongruity where every image hints at a strange and slippery insight. Each painting stands on its own, but when it is combined with the others as a single work, the viewer is compelled to search for a meaningful structure that links them. The mind seeks a narrative, but the imagery is enigmatic and skirts the edge of absurdity. There is no possible final interpretation. This approach to painting as a game stems from a desire to facilitate engagement in a culture where many are uncertain about how to view or enjoy contemporary art. In a sense, it mocks the idea of art as a grandiose, or mysterious activity.

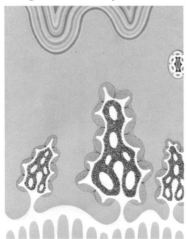

The work is also a reaction to the pressures that emerging artists experience in today's marketplace. As a long-time resident of the United States, I have become infected with the general vanity of the dreamers and go-getters of this country to create a masterpiece or "Great American Painting." And while I have no shortage of ideas, as a relatively unknown artist I have to devote a great number of hours to work other than painting in order to make a living. Additionally, there is an expectation on the part of galleries for an artist to be prolific and produce large works to command a higher price. Within these limitations, my solution to develop a significant collection of ideas was to execute them as miniatures, and then combine them into one sizable piece. But it would be dishonest to say that they would have the same impact presented individually. In this sense, the paradoxical truth about these little paintings is that they aspire to be the very thing they criticize. ❧

Luis Coig: Paintings

John Dos Passos: USA Trilogy

Pearl Abraham

He was known first as a visual artist—this was when studying all the arts was what defined a classical education. After graduating from Harvard (1916) with a degree in English, John Dos Passos went to Spain to study art and architecture. Seeing the Giotto frescoes in the Arena Chapel through sandbags piled up to prevent their destruction in the war, he worried that he and his colleagues might be the last men on earth to see these masterpieces. That night he had a sort of epiphany, realizing that "it was up to us to try and describe in colors that would not fade, our America that we loved and hated." I'm quoting from his acceptance speech for a literary honor, the 1967 Felltrinelli Prize for international distinction in literature. The title of the speech is "What Makes a Novelist."

Covering his first major NYC show in 1922 at the National Arts Club, *New York World Magazine* quoted a critic's comment on the paintings: "Hardly one of them bothers about form, but I've never seen a man have such a hell of a good time with color." This vibe of an artist having a blast also comes through in Dos Passos's writing where his joy turns infectious: you ask yourself could he, did he just

> dothat
>
>> saythat
>>
>>> breakthat

and you want him to do it again, you turn the page and find another electrifying, rulebreaking joy. This tohellwithit looseness in form for which he took criticism in his paintings became his signature,* most markedly in his *USA* trilogy, an all-inclusive mix of fact and fiction, unrestricted by

> publisherslawyers
> or anything
> or anyone

a work of biography, history, song, memoir, radio play, journalistic headlines, and more; of whatever caught his fancy, you come to appreciate.

Dos Passos knew the novel the way Cervantes did: as a powerfully fluid, expansive form capable of holding anything and everything, a kitchen-sink of a novel** with none of the paltry restrictions that today's critics and reviewers take such pride in enforcing. In an early, published collection of essays titled *Rosinante to the Road Again*, for Don Quixote's trusty steed—lean old Rosinante who resembles her master—Dos Passos celebrates both Cervantes and wandering as a way of life.

Libertarian by nature, loose and lawless in his work, Dos Passos was also footloose in his life, thinking nothing of taking a 10,000-mile trip from New York, crossing Europe all the way to the Soviet republic of Georgia, then circling through the Middle East to North Africa and back to Europe through Spain. He went wherever his intellectual curiosity directed him. He traveled by boat, train, horse-drawn carriage, camel caravan, and mail plane. He traveled all the time. And he must have written all the time because in his seventy-four years of life he produced seventeen novels, twenty-three non-fiction books, three dramas, and a book of poetry, a productive abundance that speaks for expansiveness and letting loose in both life and in literature. I may as well finish this bit of author worship with a prayer: may the book reviewers and readers of our day grow more literary and give our literature room to live and breathe. ❧

* The sentences of great writers, said William Gass, are always recognizable by the writer's signature.
** also known as Menippean satire, after the Greek cynic Menippus.

Letters on Space and Hands

Adam Day

The index finger is not the finger for pointing, something
which is dangerous, *like the odor of raisins drying
on a wicker tray.* But it is the finger for tasting
sauces and sucking; it is the finger for eating. *The only piece*

*of furniture for which Carre-Benoit felt real affection was his solid
oak filing cabinet, which he contemplated with intestinal
satisfaction whenever he passed it, especially after he found the maid
used it to store mustard, fruit salts and redcurrants, tins*

of dried onions, parsnips, coffee and lentils. In time of mourning
men make their salutations as though they were women, presenting
the right hand which covers and conceals the left, and *burial
grounds are scattered with snail shells—an allegory*

*of a grave in which man will awaken, everything breathe again, the tablecloths
whiten.* When one is to be punished *like the miller, the wind thief,
making flour from storms and knots of manure*, one uncovers the right
shoulder, revealing its odd constitution of freckles, and when one

attends a joyful ceremony, *the stove roaring in evening stillness below
the attic's bare rafters, and the linnet's nest of eight pinkish-gray eggs,*
one uncovers the left shoulder. It is by giving the leash
that possession is transferred, so goats, horses, dogs, and prisoners

of war must be presented on one *while you force yourself not to
be too much attracted to the out-of-doors.* The goat and horse
are inoffensive so may be given with the right hand *after
it has picked the dust from the cracks in the floor with a pin.* The dog

or prisoner (whose left ear must be taken) may attack, so the leash
is given—*behind dark curtains or within the clotted darkness
of the cellar's buried walls*—with the left hand to keep the right
hand ready for defense. On the other hand, *when swearing*

an oath, a bit of blood must be taken from close
to the left ear of the oath-taker, *listening to red sleeves wear out
their color*, and used to anoint the lips and sniffed.

*This poem owes a great deal to Marcel Granet and Gaston Bachelard.

Hamal
Al-Shati

Adam Day

when he was born he opened
his eyes and ass to the sea;

pares nails; pumps the priming
button on the outboard

Ibn Il-Kelb: son of a bitch; so often
his own tongue teaches him new things

he rinses his arms, feet and face
with seawater; pocketful of almonds

shrimp trawlers spew black plumes,
cantilevers clanking on the chop and swell

here if you break a bone you're done,
those aren't quite hands the bats have

the fish are beautiful; moonlight spills
a rainbow across their silver skin

we walk through green wetwhite goose
shit, pass butchers' racks: lamb flanks, hog's heads

a small shack humid with horse piss
and fish; dirty fingernails of dirty hands

I wear another man's clothes in
another man's country

offshore freighters ride at anchor
he washes his wrinkled feet, and I mine
picks small pieces of fish off the bone for me
as if I were an uncle; we wipe our lips with torn paper

gunwaled again, nets cast, tea drunk under
the Hyades; I realized people are not stones

I am uncomfortable with what I know
honestly I am uncomfortable with his teeth

and the dread of the books on my shelves
at home; what they're capable of, Hamal

a long time he's wondered how he might do it:
unhinge the wrist where it wrinkles and let go

on the wet bank the not old dog's body, sandwich
wrappers, green glass bottles throbbing in sunlight

*This poem owes a debt of gratitude to Elliott D. Woods.

Ophelia

Hannah Retzkin

My feet dangled thirty feet above the water. Darkness forgives a river's flaws. David had to convince me to climb up the railing, swing my legs over, and descend to one of the supporting beams below the bridge. One misstep, one slip, and I would hit the frigid South Platte. Deliver my body through Nebraska while my parents wept for their Ophelia. Cautiously, I lowered myself, transfixed on the rolling water.

"It would be so easy," David said.

I would just have to lean over and push myself forward to propel my body to the murk below. The river soothed me. I felt no sorrow, no suicidal wish. But I didn't trust myself. I didn't trust how easy it would be to end a life. I would fly for a brief moment before slapping the freezing water.

I was an awkward eleven year-old when the air whirled in my ears as I swung, trying to go high enough to reach a passing cloud. My friend's breathless voice was muffled as she ran across the playground. I slammed my feet against the gravel, digging my heels in hard.

"There's an ambulance outside your house. Your mom is crying in the grass."

I ran home. An empty crib. I saw her tiny summer dress on the couch. Later it was explained to me that she was stripped to be resuscitated. Natanya was buckled tight in the back seat of our minivan when she stopped breathing. Deceptively safe at home, my mother pulled open the van's door, unbuckled her from the car seat, only to find a limp body. She was gone. 9-1-1. Paramedics jumpstarted her heart but her brain was long extinguished.

The next days at the hospital I learned what adults meant when they called someone a "vegetable." I had to wash my hands before I could see Natanya. Hooked up to a respirator, wheezing mechanical breaths for her, a bag of citrine urine beside her miniature body. I held my sister one last time while lucky babes cried out to lucky mothers around me. I sung to her. I kissed her soft baby hair. I told her to "sleep tight." My mother was in the bathroom, pumping breast milk and weeping.

After she was taken off of life support, none of us could bear to sleep at home. To sleep where she had slept. In the hotel room, I curled up against my mother's chest, asking her why this had happened. She had no answers. I realized: no matter how hard I closed my eyes and wished to have my sister back, she would never return. At the funeral, my father carried her little casket in his arms, the last time he'd hold his child. He carried the casket to the little hole dug especially for her. Jewish custom allows family to help bury their loved one; I got on my knees and threw fistfuls of dirt on the plain pine box.

"It would be so easy," David said, as the water rushed below.
I nodded.
"But then you'd feel the cold." ✥

Father's Day

Joseph Scapellato

The old man went with his son to a restaurant. The restaurant was in a bowling alley where the old man used to take his son to bowl when his son was a boy. When they sat down, in a booth by the door, the old man said, "This is a terrible place to die."

The son said, "I can't believe we used to bowl here. Remember? Boy, was I lousy."

The old man didn't say anything.

"My wife is pregnant," said the son.

Their food came. It was as expected. The son paid.

Outside it was bright and clear and cool. The son, who had driven, opened the car door for the old man. The old man shuffled in and sat down. He said, "A terrible, terrible place."

The son drove the old man for a long time, for longer than it took to get to the old man's house, the house where the son had grown up. The old man grunted. He tapped the window. The son turned on news radio. They passed a chain of strip malls, a forest preserve, and three ugly rivers. The man on the radio laughed.

When they arrived at the old folks home the son opened the car door for the old man, then the door to the lobby, then the door to the receiving office, and left. A nurse, who was fat, led the old man to his room. It smelled like an airplane smells between flights. Some of the old man's things were already there: sweaters, slippers, pictures of his wife, his son, his son's pregnant wife, and the ticket from the boat that had carried the old man across the ocean from the Old Country when he'd been an infant.

The old man did not sit down. He said, "This is a terrible place to die."

The fat nurse handed him a cup of water. "All places are terrible places to die."

The old man coughed. That was how he laughed. He drank his water slowly and pointed at the bed. "All places are terrible places."

She shook her head, but in agreement. "All places are places of dying."

"But dying, dying itself is not terrible."

"Believe me," said the nurse, preparing him for his bath, "dying is terrible. Not death. Death can't be terrible."

"Nope, you've got it backwards."

The summer ended. "Tell me," said a different nurse, male, "don't you have a son?"

"You bet I have a son."

The nurse reloaded the old man's IV. "Well, won't you live on through him?"

"I want to read a book."

The nurse helped the old man into a wheelchair and pushed him to the tiny library near the cafeteria. The single bookshelf sagged with thrillers, mysteries, and romances, all donated. The room was empty.

The old man chewed his tongue.

The nurse gave him a cookie and said, "We don't disagree."

"We do disagree," said the old man five years later, seated in the cafeteria. He raised his swollen fists. "Dying isn't terrible because dying is knowable, it begins and ends, but death, death is unknowable. Therefore terrible."

This nurse, in her first week of work, laughed. She was young and skinny and she planted her hands on her hips. "Death doesn't end?"

"Right," said the old man, "only dying ends, it ends and that's that. Now how about dessert."

The next day the son returned to the old folks home with the old man's grandson, a quiet little boy. The son offered cookies his wife had baked, but the old man pretended not to smell the cookies and not to know his son and grandson and stared through their heads and chests like they were broken televisions. The son, who was sweating, told a story about this one time when they bowled together, when he was lousy. He pretended to be telling the story to the quiet little grandson but was really telling the story to the old man. He told it three times. The old man wetly cleared his throat.

When they left, the young nurse dressed the old man for bed. "Good of them to come," she said.

"Wasn't terrible. Wasn't good. But could have been either."

"It was terrible," said the nurse, crying.

"Terrible?" he said, and, not wearing any pants or underwear, touched his thigh as she watched. His thigh was soft and gray and stank like dumpsters in the sun. Then he touched hers, which was white and firm and smelled like an imaginary fruit.

"I know, I know," she said, and kissed his scalp. She kissed again.

He tried to push her. "Dying! Is! Not! Terrible!"

Ten years later the old man, bedridden, exhaled fiercely and declared: "Dying is terrible."

The young nurse wasn't young anymore. She was pregnant. "What about death."

"Death is a place."

"What kind of place."

The old man waved. "I am a place."

The summer came. The old man was very old.

The grandson returned by himself, a teenager. He looked strange, with strange hair and strange clothes.

The old man met his eyes and said, "You are strange with strange hair and strange clothes but beneath that you are a man, and beneath that you are a place, like me."

The grandson said, "Nice."

The old man grunted. Some of the tubes that were plugged into him rubbed together. "Death is a place."

The grandson gently touched the old man's arm. "We have to move you to a hospice."

"Tell me something that I do not know."

The grandson took his other hand out of his pocket and counted off on fingers: "You don't scare me; I respect you; you may know you are a place but the place itself remains unknown; the known is more terrible than the unknown; my dad won't tell us he has cancer and always wants to take us bowling but when we go he can't even throw the ball, he just starts crying and runs outside and waits in the car and when we knock on the window he gets out and pretends like he just showed up; my mom is awesome, super-awesome, she's teaching me how to bake; my girlfriend's pregnant; I'm not so sure I'm straight; today is Father's Day; happy Father's Day."

The old man coughed a real cough—it took a while, but he cleared it. "That's good," he said. "Don't go." ๛

" *Post Road* reminds me of that girl in eighth grade—the one with the chipped tooth and the precocious knowledge of drugs—who I admired in secret. It's the brilliantly strange literary journal that just might be your best friend, if you're lucky."

PAGAN KENNEDY

TREASURE ISLAND: An Appreciation

Max Grinnell

My family moved to Seattle from Madison, Wisconsin when I was nine years old, and I remember being terribly upset. What would I do in the Pacific Northwest, away from my friends? I would also be quite distant from the many pleasure of Wisconsin Dells, with its multitude of water parks and low-rent haunted houses.

My mother reminded me of my many books, and I was promised several new books upon our arrival in Seattle. She knew me well, and the promise of more books was certainly enough to occupy my thoughts on the long Amtrak ride from Madison to Seattle.

When we arrived in Seattle, there were in fact new books already waiting for me. My grandfather had sent along a collection of Great Illustrated Classics. These books were essentially illustrated Cliff Notes for juveniles, as they resembled the garden variety comic book. As I made my first foray into this trove, I passed over *The Scarlet Pimpernel* ("What's a pimpernel?") and *The Man in the Iron Mask* ("Is this like Iron Maiden?") and settled on *Treasure Island*.

Treasure Island sounded good from the start. First there was "treasure" in the title, which implied some type of great wealth, potentially in the form of gold, gold, and more gold. Then there was the word "island." I had not done much traveling by age nine (no Geneva, Switzerland, just Lake Geneva, Wisconsin) and so I remember thinking, "There must be travel involved. I want to travel."

I opened this Treasure Island-lite and I found a map. Could it be? By this point in my life, I had already spent many hours drawing my own maps that detailed the location of hidden treasure in our front yard and fantastical war-room style military maps that detailed the struggle, a dream-battle between the Evil Empire (in the Darth Vader fashion) and G.I. Joe. I looked closely and saw names like "Spyglass Hill," "Skeleton Island," and finally "BULK OF TREASURE HERE," finished with a large "X." This R.L. Stevenson knew me, I could tell, or at least he shared a love of maps and buried treasure.

As I started to read, I was drawn in by the language and in particular, the description of Billy Bones as "a tall, strong, heavy, nut-brown man; his tarry pigtail falling over the shoulders of his soiled blue coat; his hands ragged and scarred, with black, broken nails; and the saber cut across one cheek, a dirty, livid white." I remember thinking that I was terrified after reading this. "Who is this man?," I thought. "Is he insane? Why is his cut white?" I paused a moment to think about all of this before eagerly continuing on.

Over the next few pages, Bones proceeds to meet the whole family at the Admiral Benbow Inn, including Jim Hawkins, the young boy and sometimes hero of this tale. I remember being very envious of this Jim fellow, as he got to help out Bones with all sorts of errands. Would I have fetched a tankard of rum for him? In a heartbeat. Keep my "weather-eye open for a seafaring man with one leg?" If only we had such characters in our bland 1970s apartment building! I could have done without some of Bones' less savory habits, like yelling out sea shanties and slapping his hands on the table, but that all seemed like a small price to pay for such excitement and intrigue.

I made a habit of trying to work the lingua franca of *Treasure Island* into my conversations at this point, with little success. Enamored of nautical terms like "old salt" and "true sea dog," I felt that I could bring these key phrases into the everyday life of Madrona Elementary School. Suffice it to say, an inner-city school in Seattle near the conclusion of the 20th century was probably not the best place for such an experiment. The setting was less than ideal (no boats and not many sailor-types in my school) and it was the wrong century.

After finishing this comic-book version of *Treasure Island*, I picked up the real deal and read it in an evening while thinking about my own potential future, which would hopefully involve buried treasure, colorful old salts, and a largely benign and peaceful form of piracy. I was in the wrong century once again, of course, but I still dream of moments where I am wandering around Spyglass Hill, hiding in an apple barrel, or in a battle of wits with Long John Silver. Since reading *Treasure Island* for the first time twenty-five years ago, I have met a few Billy Bones-esque characters and I hope to meet many more. ❧

A Plea to My Vegan Great-grandchildren

A.M. Juster

It is my hope you will agree
I lacked responsibility
for disco, Vista and *The View*;
consider me a victim too.
I wasn't all that keen on war
or most oppression of the poor,
and please believe that I regret
your payments on our Chinese debt.
Oh sure, I looked the other way
from toxic waste and Tom DeLay,
but I still paid most bills on time
and uncut nosehair's not a crime.
I know you hate the meat I ate,
but bacon always tasted great
and barbecue, when smoked just right
was such a sensual delight
...though now I'm being more objective
and see it from the pig's perspective.
Despite these sordid legacies,
can't you condone some eggs and cheese?
Perhaps for some unique occasion?
You may require more persuasion,
so I will make my best defense:
for all my sins I had the sense
to marry someone, I would guess,
who balanced my genetic mess
and made you brilliant, strong and kind—
and sensitive where I was blind—
so muster Wiccan charity
and try not to disparage me.

My Billy Collins Moment

A.M. Juster

for Midge Goldberg

For no reason I can think of,
I thought I would write a poem,
but it seemed
nothing urgent needed to be said,
so I started to wonder
about *Playboy* bunnies,
then, after a long interval
of hardly thinking at all,
it struck me how strange it was
that a man should build his empire
of nubile women
wearing cotton on their *derrieres*
and fake rabbit ears
erect above their long, lush hair.

Of course, speaking for myself,
I am not turned on
by thoughts of sex with *faux* animals,
no matter how cuddly they might be,
let alone those known to harbor
ticks with Lyme Disease
and similar parasites in their fur.
For that matter, if called to action,
I would prefer pan-fried *lapin*,
although I tend to be nonjudgmental
about the tastes of others
and often feel I should give up
meat altogether.

Having no more of a conclusion,
I ponder

whether I should be writing
to their editors
about my perspective
or composing a *cri de cœur*
to someone on their board.

Maybe, at the least,
I should be getting back to that poem.

Bubbie

Robert Pack

My first raw book of poems had just come out;
Exalted by my words upon a printed page,
I borrowed my stepfather's car
To drive to Brooklyn where I gave a copy
To my uncle Phil, my mother's sister, Pearl,
And grieving grandmother who had
Moved in with them when Grandpa died
Quite suddenly, though he had not been sick
One single day of his extended life.
The family had been compelled to flee
From Russia to escape the wild pogroms,
The horseback Cossacks charging down the hill
And splintering their windows and their doors.

Asked to recite some of my poems,
I sat down with them in the dining room
With küchen freshly made by grandmother,
And I intoned my yearning cadences.
But Grandma couldn't follow them
In the American vernacular, so uncle Phil
Translated them into the Yiddish
Grandma understood. And when
I read a poem about my father's heart attack
And mother's fear of loneliness,
The tears cascaded down my Bubbie's cheeks
As they applauded me and asked for more.

Opponent of the Czar, Phil had evaded
The pursuit of the police, crossing the border
Just ahead of them at night, and now
He was reduced to selling women's clothes—
The price of freedom that he had to pay.
Pearl could intone long passages
Of Pushkin deep from childhood memory
And sing old ballads of the working poor.

Grandma was always in the kitchen,
Wooden stirring spoon in hand,
Concocting the world's lightest matzo balls,
Gefilte fish, and pastries, küchen
For her daughter's appetite for sweets.
    Is this a scene that even long-lived love
Cannot prevent from windy vanishing—
The table with its blue ceramic vase
Of purple flowers all forgotten and
With everybody gone? Yet, Bubbie, here's
Another poem for you, the taste
Of küchen still upon my lips—as if
Your Yiddish heart might still be listening.

Power

Robert Pack

They're gone, the powers that I once possessed—
Control of lightning bolts and hurricanes;
Old age does that: fatigue, and care, and stress.
Accepting loss, my last strength, still remains.

One summer night when my first son was four,
A storm came up and frightened him from sleep;
I picked him up, since hugs alone could cure
All aches and sorrows in those days and keep

Him safe from harm, carried him to our den,
And sat him snugly in a chair with me.
We watched a streaking lightning bolt break free
Across the range of snow-tipped mountain peaks,

And, shuddering against my shoulder then,
He said to me, "Again, do that again!"

Saro's Love Song

Joseph Bottum

On May 6, 2010, the body of Zardasht Osman, a twenty-three-year-old
journalist who wrote under the name "Saro Zardasht," was found in Arbil,
the capital of Kurdistan. He had been kidnapped and murdered after
writing exposés of the ruling party, led by Kurdish president Masud
Barzani. Earlier in the year, Saro had written a comic, almost Beat-style
tirade about Barzani, from which these English tetrameters are loosely
drawn

I am in love with Masud's daughter—
Masud Barzani: the man you see
here and there, the man who says
he is my president. I want
him for my father-in-law. I want
his son for my brother-in-law. I want
his lovely daughter to marry me.

If I were married to Masud's daughter,
we'd spoon and honeymoon in Paris.
We'd visit her uncle's American mansion.
We'd leave my room in the backstreets of Arbil
for an upmarket place in Sari Rash—
patrolled by fierce American dogs
and grim Israeli bodyguards.

If I were married to Masud's daughter,
I'd name my little brother as head
of special forces—the luckless boy
who's finished school but can't find a job
and talks about leaving Kurdistan.
I'd put my ancient father in charge
of all our Kurdish militia troops.

If I were married to Masud's daughter,
my mother would have Italian doctors
nodding wisely while she moaned

about her feet and swollen heart.
My uncles would have swank offices.
My nieces and nephews would all get rich
as high officials for the state.

My friends say, Saro, let it go.
You've never even seen the girl
you babble about so much of the time.
The Barzanis, old Mustafa's tribe—
they can kill whenever they want.
And you'll be what they want to kill,
if you don't shut up about their daughter.

But why should I be silent now?
My father warred against Saddam
with Masud's brother—I swear on his knife:
three nights on the mountain they stood together.
Masud says he's my president,
but when did he last leave his palace
to visit old soldiers in Arbil's slums?

I wonder what my mother-in-law
looks like. On the Internet
with only a few clicks you can find
photos of other leaders' wives—
but never Masud's. Is she shy?
Without knowing, I can't decide
who should help arrange my marriage.

At first, I thought I would take an imam
with me—a good, respectable figure—
and a few of those old militiamen,
to ask for the hand of Masud's daughter.
But everyone says I must use instead
some of Saddam's collaborators,
the murderers and ethnic cleansers

that Masud now seems to like so much.
Or maybe my busy brother-in-law
will mention me in a press release
so my father-in-law can learn who I am.
Or maybe that pop-star Dashne will sing
about my love for Masud's daughter.
She's always around the Barzanis these days.

I am in love with Masud's daughter—
Masud Barzani: the man you see
here and there, the man who says
he is my president. I want
him for my father-in-law. I want
his son for my brother-in-law. I want
his lovely daughter to marry me.

A Vision of India

Whitney Dubie

And all is vanity, vanity. The cry of Ecclesiastes that came
long before the building of the tall, stone statue of Buddha
that once stood as a symbol of peace in the middle of the green lake
in Hyderabad, where day after day they dumped truckloads
of shit into the thick, muddy water as women in red and grey saris

washed their long, ink-black hair. And while we slept on the train
with the stars and wind coming through the barred windows, someone
was planting a bomb in Charminar's ancient walls, the white marble
falling like thousands of choked birds in the smoldering night
even as the cockroaches swarmed our sleeping heads.

After we learned of the bombing, we stayed three days by the blood-
red Indian Ocean, watching the distant ships from Dakar with their spices
and oil, then turned to that overgrown field between our two stone houses.
Stepping through snake dens, I lifted my skirt to race through the tall
olive grass, cutting my legs as the thin blood fell.

That morning, long before the sun had managed to climb up over
the endless oceans of field and earth in Bapatla, we worked in the black
garden, uprooting potato leeks under a damp April sky.
Afterwards, drinking coffee mixed with goat's milk and cane sugar,
we watched the mango trees swaying in the late-afternoon wind

and thought of how strange and dream-like our young lives were,
of the simplicity of our hands working the soil. Listening to the news
on your rust-burnt radio cutting in and out in the sweltering night,
the images of blood-stained marble, bodies, and the weary eastern light…
it seems we are always working for something. And now the white

pieces of Charminar fall like dominos or the wings of falling birds, to be gathered in a burning heap, all in the name of some impossible ideal—the leaving behind of the body, the abandonment of the soul, compelling us at last to purify ourselves as best we could, as we lay down by the edge of that thick, green lake to bury the remains of Buddha and of Charminar in the deep, damp earth.

The Guinness at Tigh Mholly

Angela Alaimo O'Donnell

Yer makin' the Yanks' Tour, are ye?
Peadar said, Cian smiling behind the bar
pouring 4 pints for his new American friends,

our 100-mile drive from Kerry to here
amusing to a man for whom the next
county is another country away.

He told us the history of the pub,
the clock that stopped at Mholly's birth
a century gone, ticked past the time

while he walked us from stone room to stone room
naming the faces in the Stations on the walls,
a Celtic Virgil leading a misguided tour.

All the while we drank the famous Guinness
drawn from Mholly's lines laid long ago
making it the best on the Spidéil Road,

while we argued poetry, Barack O'Bama,
the slant of the light on Connemara cliffs,
no new thing fine as the old.

What he knew he knew sure as his own hand
and wouldn't take *no* for an answer:
Heaney was a hack, Donegal men dishonest,

and Clifden as far as you'll need to go
should you need to leave home for awhile
and you know you'll be needing to come back.

A Kind of Ductility

Simone Kearney

Now it is January, I've nothing to do.
Everything is purple, predictable
as grass, the way it is known to grow
an inch a year in some colder climates.
The rate of hair growth differs in each individual.
I don't tell you this. I hum to myself instead,
folding newspapers, napkins, dresses.
I brush my hair because it is growing long.
You thank me for the small landscape
I left on your window.
I wait by the wardrobe.
Your ears are blossoms,
so full as to burst.
It's as if a feather were loosed
across our faces
for the purpose of laughter.
But we grew serious,
rebuffed the lettuce wilting in the kitchen,
& the parakeet in the living room. I have a shawl
to my mouth
to stop the leaves
from falling. Puccini plays in the background.
All I have in my hand
is a semi-world in the shape of a telephone,
and a quietness approaching a seed. So
I stroll along the melon grave.
I wanted to call it a grove.
I wait by the water fountain now,
flat-ribbed against the grinding shale. I emerge
only slightly.
Is that my breathing blending with the rocks?
How quiet the wind is.

Morning

Simone Kearney

Light gives
nothing back. Cold fills
the gaps.
Noise
the thread of some argument
I can't catch—
I'm always entering into
the conversation
halfway. Just leave
me out next time. The delicious expectation of
no one, nestling the throat
of silence.

Outside stands
for something I don't know, won't
make a symbol of. The squeal of the train—
push back
thoughtfulness—
leave it out—
the window cut in half and me
measured in quantities of
partial blue and off-
white. I tell you I don't want
any of it. Sun
wants
the eyes of everything,
enormous holes. Sun
casts me exotic,
an unavoidable
sensation of being
looked
at, crystallized.

I'm
mortified by the clarity
of these operations.
Not to be propped
on light,
not to be made in relation to,
diagonal
to, halfway towards.

Better, to be indefinite, not
to take shape.

I don't want
my body back.
Take it away with you, sun, why
don't you?

When Asked to Explain the Fall of Mankind

Hannah Armbrust

For Emma from the Orvieto Duomo Façade

The Duomo façade pushes into Orvietani sky and continues
till my neck aches and my eyes crawl ant-like up
and down this jigsaw, which is what we
were doing, the rug rolled back, the pieces spread
across the oak floor, when you asked, *Why
is man inherently bad?* I had no answer
for your unsettling nine-year-old eyes.
Perhaps perplexity is the fruit of the Fall.

The sun lengthens over carvings where the tree of life
casts spider shadows. In the piazza, a man, his back
bent, circles round and round on a bike. Its chain
ticks hollow as a snake's rattle. His corduroy
pants are dark and rich as the ground that God molded
into Adam. *And it was good*, like the day you, my sister,
were born—smooth, red, and damp. My finger slid
easy over your face, into your new hands aglow
with morning light, and I could not believe in a Fall.

I see it above me chiseled in marble
and it's disconcerting. The snake grins like a secondhand
car salesman, a sidewalk clown, or pickpocket illusionist.
Wind begins while shadows crawl up the steps
where children twist like vehement ants and Cain, arm
curved, beats Abel to the ground. Soon blood
will steep the dirt around his head, a sticky, dark orange
like those egg yolks I broke the morning your twin brother,
his face twisted hard, tackled you into the ground, your hair
in his fist. He grinned and his stick curved like a snake
about to strike. You screamed and the stick made a dull,
flat sound against your head. I could not understand.

A terrible determination glints in Cain's
eyes, the same look you had when (only weeks
after your own beating) you trapped
our rabbit in its cage and pelted it with stones,
while it cowered and screamed. You watched
it scuttle back and forth with an eerie twist
at the corners of your mouth. I grabbed your face
and shook you too hard. We have both fallen.

The Setting Evening

Stuart Krimko

As a sun sets, so does
darkness. Towards morning
stars disappear and
then the dark begins to,
replaced by light of
a more general sort than stars.
What happens next
is that eyes open, like
points beyond stars, that
dark, so they accept what
the sun gives them. Sure,
the sun is a star too, but
a different sort of star, a
likely star, familiar, the kind
that stays put even
though it moves, cycles. Stars
cycle too, collect in
pictograms or portraits of fate,
but they rotate in unison,
a flock of far-off jellyfish.
Neither sun nor flock
completely disappears.
When one is triumphant
the other swims below
the horizon, a picture
across the lateral expanse
of both eyes; and when
eyes close, to blink perhaps,
the line is cut and this
is when for once there is
nothing, for one brief citation
of eradicated bliss; and then
to dream, to rest, they

invent a continuum
derived in part from this
and in part from full sight,
from knowing everything,
how everything works. Sense
splashes on a deeply
noncommittal screen, and
sometimes sticks, but mostly,
so experts say, it's
whisked away to a
troubled world of forgotten
touches, how one
distant star became our sun,
and another another,
its long-lost brother.

Self-Portraits

Stuart Krimko

I have too many words in my pocket,
too many tunes. The pocket sags and
then the pants. The shirt is untucked,
the shirt becomes unbuttoned, soon
it's my bare chest exposed to the world.

I have too many considerations, my
mind goes dizzy thinking about them,
it spins and whirs and wishes it was
in some other skull. My considerations
are offered to the air at market value
but the air sends them back.

I have too many temptations, too
many counterparts, too many doppelgangers,
too many delights and too many
pretensions, I have too many
poems and too many self-portraits.
I have too many petals and not enough
flowers.

I have too many obvious advantages.
It's difficult to make sense of the world
without the attendant hardships to make
it mean something. If only I could make
things more difficult for myself, if only
I wasn't so steeped in excess. If only
I had less.

Reasons to Search for Earth-like Planets

Will Dowd

—A poem sent on the Kepler spacecraft, currently circling the Sun.

Because the people here
are buying abstract paintings
daubed by Asian elephants.

Because they like Shakespeare
but prefer their drama
caught on hidden camera.

Because somewhere out there,
among the ringworm of spiral galaxies,
amid the crushed cereal puffs of star clusters,
there must be an audience for poetry.

Take this message to the sun:
someday I will make it off this rock
if I have to cling to the back of a satellite
or stow away aboard a space-bound sonnet.

Ascension in the Uffizi Courtyard

Will Dowd

Feeling feverish in Florence, I am of two minds over certain
things, like how I could be both wedged
in line outside the Uffizi and hovering over the street
artists tossing off charcoal cherubs, the tourists licking stubs
of melted gelato. The air shimmers, the heat
vapors off stone. My body below refuses to budge.
It holds out for chilled galleries, the Madonnas caged
in gold-leaf, the infant who strains in their anemic
arms, fumbling for traction on their silk terrain.
He hasn't made it very far since birth. He rubs
their neck and cheeks with his starfish hands,
starved for some response to his millennial colic—
a hum through pressed lips, a snapped tongue cluck—
anything to be reminded, once again, where he stands.

Pavor Nocturnus with Relativity

Bianca Stone

"Item I gyve unto my wief my second best bed."
—*William Shakespeare's will*

I have to divide into sections
of visibility. The deciduous
flowering shrubs can only
ape the words *I love you*
so many times before
they burst into flames. Soon
we'll go to Chinatown
and buy unusual vegetables,
cook them however we please.
7.3 billion years later and this
theory prevails—that we are
constant and independent
of our own energy, our
affection autonomous
from any other movement.
Breaking it down onto
the smallest scale, even
in your gravitational pull
I could say anything I wanted
lying beside you
on the second best bed.
A wire begins at the sternum
and moves into an alternate sternum.
When I close my eyes I can see
a wolf eating an old wolf
in the blue evening.
Repotting the braided bonsai tree
is not something you just do.
You have to understand
how to control something.

You have to understand
what something is.

Someone Will Have to Tell You

Bianca Stone

Someday soon you will let your hair grow
and look like everyone else. And let there be a kingdom
alongside the kingdom and a forsythia alongside you.
Your mother has walked out of all her pictures

into the ether. There is hair in envelopes and the hair
in lockets and the hair growing
in graves. Saints are kneeling over your portrait.
The stratocumulus clouds are forming
in your chest. Fog around your feet.

You'll have to listen to the bananas peeling.
Listen to your books on tape. Little by little
your face will float away
from your other face.

Someday you won't know what to eat. Someone
will have to tell you. Someone will have to carry you
into the back yard so you can hear the Canadian geese
rise hysterically from the river.

The Argument

Adam Fitzgerald

The life we didn't live.
The time tepid as bronze.
The stacked air. The frozen rail.
The dripping of blue drops in summer.
The honey-trees, the brick façade,
the empty canyons of light
between Ferry Street and birch leaves
where a cloud drops a sock.

The sky. The records of clocks.
The wooden hours. The fort postcards.
The salvoes of breakfast paper
on exhibit somewhere.

The gears inert. The girls inanimate.
The dolly. The one side of a house,
the other four stories high.
The weave of poor shoals.
The hoops of brittle violets.
The tubing of cubed lilacs.
The floorboards of the ocean.
The single step. The fourteen feet.
The oblong rooms of moss.
The apples. The cherries. The feathers.
The straw. The manure. The dirt.
The difficult gardens of your eyes.
The small fruits. The rubber necktie.
The sour voice. The nowhere special.
The lilting train. The old Queen.
The different kinds of musk and night.

The wind to tell us who we are.
The sloop of our look. The departing.
The advanced trust. The desires.
The mistress. The bus. The come-hither sleep.
The day. The hour. The Highlands.
The liberal miles of marsh grass. The leaves.
The leave-taking. The place. The sun.
The succession of rain. The decrepitude.

The refrain. The song.
The meadow of the wind.
The meadow in the wind.
The hired passage. And yesterday,
the lying down to recover breath.
The argument. The raiment. The tune.
The rust. The tributes of lost tribes.
The great minds of small force.
The tempest. The sleights. The self.
The valley covered in stars.

Proud Hand

Adam Fitzgerald

There are few cliffs here but the largess of cold hours.
Lightness of breath maintains the western skies.
Winter, painters, this marble path . . .
What else calls to a carpet of bees, and burnt air?

Child of the wind-honored Yucatan, the sea's feet
are your unhappy exhibition. The prospecting pictures
grow, but gravity grows too, steep as blue
sea-salt, red as the gummed grass of wildflowers.

Prelusion

Allison Power

for David Blasco

In Rome the arches are upside down
Caveats I recognize
Sdoppiare means something
To disconnect or open outward
And your runny nose over the hash browns
An oculus admits the only light
Sympathy for the pilgrims,
The Cathars, and Mary Todd
Beneath the rotunda
There's a slab of marble rose
In the way we experience nausea
But it was more song and dance
My childhood, a few tree trunks,
And an elevator ride in style
If I were someone else
I was here a moment ago
Tipping an urn

The Futurists

Allison Power

Please don't talk about yourself
or the way you feel.

I write a postcard from the trees.
I'm the owl. You're the Tibetan goat

building bright shadows. It's 1983.
We remove dust jackets to make blankets.

I sneeze clumsily. The windows are the same
coasts regenerating at my feet. In the lab

the mice are abnormally small.
They ask questions about sex.

The heat changes from yellow to blue.
The sink is full. With intentions to be genuine,

to mean what we said, we scale the shelves
for paper towels then peter out

in mattresses. I pull another blanket
over the big garden. You stick out your tongue

and write to me. Did you know the Futurists
constructed a life-size and edible sculpture

of a female body made of meats and grains?

The Visitor

Tryfon Tolides

Korifi Voiou, Greece

Stay long enough, until the sun and blue seep in.
Until the people no longer seem exotic fixtures. Until you bow
with astonishment from the persistence and strangeness
of their lives. Until you feel right in abandoning them for walks
in the mountains and in the night fog, alone. Stay
until you hear the church bell in the fog.
Until you come home to the same few plates and small frying pan,
day after day, until the table becomes simple. Until you learn
to calibrate the ash in the stove so the wood lasts
longer and the fire still burns when you return.
Stay until the stars and mountains, the air and falling down stone
houses become facts of your blood. Stay until you are here.

Watching the Light

Tryfon Tolides

Houston, Texas

To sit and watch the light is a good discipline.
Practically nothing happens.

A gray bird with a longish tail;
white and black around its wings; black beak; dark
or black around its eyes. I could smell its soul if it let me
just put my nose to its breast. I see the shape
of its breast and wonder how my palm could
come to know that; a wind inside me takes on the shape
and sets something aglow with roundness.

The bird has come near me. We are both in the sun.
The sun goes behind clouds, comes back. We are aware
of each other. As to the purpose of our meeting,
it is a secret peace march.

The wind smells like autumn, like a city street.
Clouds, blue sky, leafless trees, and our shadows
against the golden light. The train rumbling. The whistle.

Even if something like loneliness is present. God
or the world or the kernel inside me is brought to rest.
Even as the hells continue.

Because of a leaf scraping and dancing and tumbling across
the parking lot, the parking lot becomes a temple.

And now one last train, the last light on the dull yellow
locomotive. The moving boxcars in the last golden light,
like a memory or something yet to come. Almost
gone. Then gone.

For Who Knows How Long

Tryfon Tolides

Hartford, Connecticut

I make my hands into the shape
of a trapping prayer
and on my knees,
lean toward the grasshopper,
wanting to feel
its springing kicks
and pulses, to hold its life
by the sides between my fingers.
I miss it once, find it again,
and descend my domed palms
over God's green
machinery. As I close my fingers
around it, the grasshopper
flies out through a hole
without touching me.
Now I must wait again
for this sensation
of childhood, the huts on hills
of my village, the tall dry grasses,
the taste of *ksinotiri*, sour cheese,
for who knows how long.

Self-Portrait, Number 1 (Shanghai, Winter 2008)

Katherine Lien Chariott

Jianguo West Road, Lane 212, Number First, Room 401

Backgrounds are easier, so let's begin with this room, cold and quiet and still. Take in all that you can in five seconds and then close your eyes.

Did you see? Do you remember?

1. the green chaise lounge to your left, elegant in shape, but obviously cheap
2. the black recliner and footrest across from it—Ikea, of course
3. the rounded orange chair in the far corner, with its stained yellow cushion
4. the blond wood folding table at the end of the room
5. the black wire chair in front of that table
6. the stained red of the floor, such a beautiful color

Open your eyes now and look again. Keep looking, this time, and you will see:

1. a pile of clothes in the corner next to that orange and yellow chair (those sad-rags looking humble, even punished; that chair looking, somehow, stern, like the author of that punishment)
2. one black boot, size 38, with its heel broken off, just under that table, trying to hide its own loss, its own lack, its own shame
3. the overflowing trash can by the recliner, a mess of bottles, of cans, of cigarette ends, all of them wanting to escape back into the room
4. shards of glass glinting danger all across that red floor, challenging you to deny, to me, to yourself, that they were scattered there on purpose to reflect its beautiful color
5. the door, on the other side of that table, opening onto the balcony, and the man standing beyond it, looking out at the clouds of dust all around him (oh this polluted, beautiful place)
6. the city itself, just past him, darkened by its own dirt, by its sorrow at facing the day

See what that man sees (the dim outline of skyscrapers, the white tiles smooth under his feet, the edge of a faded red curtain, the more beautiful red of that floor) as he moves from outside to in, as he takes his seat at that table, and surveys the room. See with him:

1. the white walls on all sides, paint cracked and chipping, wearing you out
2. the open, indecent closet, overflowing with junk, but every hanger bare

3. that green chaise lounge where I normally sit (it is forlorn without me)

4. the yellow wood of the table before him, covered with tissues that look like flowers and cotton balls and trash, all of them soaked in blood, some of it dark and dried and some of it fresh and wet just come out of a body

5. a flash of movement as I enter the room, only to stop just inside it, fingers nervously twisting the cloth of the skirt I still wear, though it is torn on one side, a victim of the night

6. the comfort of darkness as he closes his eyes, hoping to think about nothing

Now, come towards me, come to me, to stand with me and in me. See the room, once again, see with my eyes:

1. my poor black boot, heartbreaking in its singleness, heartbroken at the loss of its partner, of its own heel. It spreads itself out on the floor defiantly, making me remember how shiny (and proud) it looked that afternoon when I bought it, bargained down to 100 yuan, the shopkeeper frowning as she packed up the box, and him at my side, shaking his head

2. my black tights spread-eagled over the back of that green lounge, as if trying to make up (lewdly, shamelessly) for what I'd rather deny

3. that man at the table, bent over so his hair hangs over one eye, almost covering the purple blooming around it, that purple that makes him look like he did that night (a lifetime ago) when he came home after losing a fight, and I spent the whole night holding his hands, the same ones that sit in his own lap now, holding each other

4. the sun working to brighten the sky outside to blue, but failing to do more than lighten the blackness to grey, just as I have failed so many times to do more than I do at this moment: open my mouth and then close it again in silence, in disappointment, when I was so sure that this was the day I would finally find the words that could make myself seen ❧

KAMBY BOLONGO MEAN RIVER by Robert Lopez

Matt Bell

When I look back at the reading I did in 2009, it's mostly the short story collections I remember, for whatever reason. The one exception is Robert Lopez's *Kamby Bolongo Mean River*, the book that beat all other books for me that year. I was lucky enough to get to read the book in galleys, then again on its release date in October, and then a third time in December. Since then, it's become a book that constantly haunts my desk, no matter how many times I try to return it to the shelves. There's so much to admire about the book, from its formal elements—it's written in short, beautiful paragraphs, full of repetition and empty of commas—to its fantastic narrator, a character in possession of one of the most uniquely rendered and affecting modes of speech in recent memory.

Kamby Bolongo Mean River is narrated by a young man under observation, trapped in what is probably a hospital room that contains only a bed and a telephone. He begins his story focused on the telephone: "Should the phone ring I will answer it. I will say the hello how are you and wait for a response. I will listen to what the person on the other end says. I will listen to the words."

He says, "The trouble is some people use words one way but other people use those words a different way altogether. My problem is I think about one word too long."

He says, "A word like injury can split your head open."

The narrator does answer this phone frequently, but usually the callers have the wrong number, or at least the narrator thinks so. In between phone calls, he draws stick figures of his life-story on the walls, masturbates compulsively, and tells us the the story of his childhood. What we are told, in halting steps frequently interrupted by narrative tangents and linguistic diversions, is that the narrator grew up in Injury, Alaska, with his brother Charlie and his mother. That his mother was frequently out of work, fired alternately because she wouldn't work overtime and because she wouldn't sleep with her bosses. That his brother Charlie wanted to be a boxer or an actor. That their mother often fed them sandwiches and coleslaw. That she got both the brothers singing lessons but that the narrator was the better singer, so much better that Charlie often punched the narrator in the stomach so he would "stop singing and dancing better than him," and that once, Charlie and the narrator "sang a song about the kamby bolongo," a song for which he and Charlie "had made up the song and the lyrics were the best [they'd] done."

Through the story, these details and many others repeat themselves, take on larger and larger significances even as the narrator's utterances undercut the ground the reader is left to stand on, offering facts that seemingly cannot be factual then attaching them to emotions that ring startlingly true, until it becomes clear that, as the narrator claims, it is not the content that is most important but the delivery.

The narrator says, "If you concentrate on the words you lose the voice and the voice is too important to lose. How the voice pronounces each word is probably the most important thing."

He says, "The words themselves are important less than half the time."

He says, "It's always better to listen to the voice and leave the words alone."

The story of *Kamby Bolongo Mean River* is nearly all remembered, a childhood recalled rather than experienced, but the book never suffers for this backward stance, as so many others might. Because of the unique voice of the narrator and the recursive undermining of his speech, Lopez is able to move forward by moving backward first, looping through the unsteady past to create the headlong future. It is probably fair to say that the past of the novel's last third is hardly the past of the novel's first, but even this shifting narrative feels truer of life than many more grounded tellings captured in other novels.

In the end, the narrator tells us, "I think I have lived an entire life beside the point," but perhaps he is wrong. After all, it is not what the narrator has done—or what has been done to him—that creates the emotional resonance of this deeply sad, deeply moving book, but rather the way in which it is told. In *Kamby Bolongo Mean River*, Robert Lopez has created a character imbued with a tireless voice, who speaks with "nothing impeding [himself] from [himself]," so that eventually his speech exhausts the elements of his own story, causes them to break down, to shift, to realign themselves into new stories created not by deception but by trauma. By the end of the novel, the narrator is still in the same place he was at the beginning, but I am willing to bet that no reader—no listener, for this novel is as much spoken as it is written—will be able to say the same. Despite the claims of the narrator, these words do matter, and it's the many talents of Robert Lopez that made them so. This is a novel no one should miss. ❧

Davey

Jesse Cataldo

Sara took the rest of the cigarette from her mouth and crushed it, grinding the lit end into the windowsill. Regretting the mess, she slid her thumb across the small pile of ash.

"Four hours," she heard her mother say through the phone, "when I expect you to arrive at 6:30 and then it's four hours before I hear a word I begin to get worried. I don't think this is anything out of the ordinary."

"Three hours," Sara answered. "I got in late and I've been on the phone with you for twenty minutes. It's three hours if you add it up."

"Hours alone is too long. I don't want to hear hours. I want minutes."

"I am fine," she said, putting equal stress on each word.

"Now you are. Two hours ago who knows. You could be in a ditch somewhere with your head removed."

She looked over to the closet, where she had thrown her bag. It was sticking halfway out, something yellow caught in the teeth of the zipper. She could not imagine what this was.

There was a balance to the hotel room she had not expected. Two beds, two end tables, two lamps, and a television square in the middle. Below the first bed was a vent for the central air and she was sure there was another one, somewhere, because of the draft she could feel blowing around her toes. Something about this kind of symmetry seemed stifling.

The hotels she was used to were never so exact, motels with thin metal railings and ragged-edged ping pong tables, dusty resorts propped up on the rims of national parks. They had never taken city vacations. Her father hated cities. Instead they pushed in the other directions, spending weekends in reclaimed log cabins, formerly crumbling, on the banks of sick lakes filled with green moss. These were expansion trips, as her father sometimes called them, where she would learn just how much more there was outside the things she saw every day. But the world she found was surprisingly vacant, lonely, cold fields pawing at the highway as they drove through the night. People arguing in the parking lots of rest-stop diners. In a small town in west Pennsylvania she saw the moon rise like a dirty dish and cried in the car, almost to herself, after a legless man asked her for a cigarette.

They had tried once, when she was eight, to visit DC, in part for a school project where she needed to learn three things about George Washington. This was the time she had made a scrapbook of sights with empty spaces to put her own pictures. Instead they got stuck in traffic. Her parents argued about parking spaces. She fell asleep in the backseat and woke up back at home, in her own bed, with no memory of how she'd gotten there.

"What did you eat?" her mother said, "assuming that you did eat. And please don't tell me crackers."

This hotel was different. There were thick ferns in the lobby, fake hibiscus in tall, patterned vases, and a bartender who looked like he might play Santa Claus in a different season. "These April nights," he said, shaking his head as he poured her soda, "oh, these April nights," and she liked it, although she didn't understand what he meant. This was a hotel meant for people, for people on their way to places, not a set for a TV movie about broken dreams.

Entering the room, she had turned both lamps on and then one off and then on again. She flipped the hassock from the easy chair with one foot and righted it back with the other. The design of the room was curt, soft-spoken, its pastel walls suggesting soft pillows and reasonable rates. She unpacked. Outside the cars came and went, and she realized that from the seventh floor you could not see much of anything. "You wouldn't believe the things," her mother said, "the things you find in those hotel ice machines. It's enough to make you sick." She held the phone away from her ear and stood between the two beds, imagining one side of the room as a mirror image of the other.

Her father had booked the room for the two of them but was now stuck overnight in Manassas, the victim of an early spring blizzard that was "crippling the Eastern Seaboard." These were his words, delivered with the throaty assurance of someone quoting a weatherman. They had spoken briefly through airport telephones, hers spackled with the white ghosts of chewed Wrigley's, a strange counterpoint to the cleanliness of the terminal. Later he wired her one hundred dollars and a note. *Sara darling please be good and for God's sake do not tell your mother* it read.

"I'd feel better if I heard you chewing."

"You're making this worse," Sara said, "you're making this much, much worse."

"I'm sorry," her mother answered, "I don't mean to be a harpy and I don't want to ruin your trip but you know how you are."

She did. Sara was flighty, unfocused, prone to broken curfews and eyeglasses lost in unfamiliar glove compartments. Her relationship with her mother was one of continuous growth; they enlarged each others faults, catapulting failures back and forth until her mother was an unrepentant nag and she a constant disappointment. In reality, they were civil and sometimes loving and were following two television shows regularly. The first, on Sundays, about a Missouri family's booming veterinary practice. The second, on Wednesdays, following a dissipated clan of expatriate teenagers living in an Alsatian hunting lodge.

"How are you otherwise. No men leering at you, I hope."

"There are no men. Not that kind. They all have uniforms. They seem professional."

"That's how it starts. Uniforms and the charm and then what."

"Mom, this is the greatest hotel ever," she exclaimed, a falsely childish ring in her voice, "they have four Jacuzzis. Four Jacuzzis and a bar that serves chartreuse. Chartreuse, mom." Her mother loved chartreuse. Consuming things with secret recipes was one of the few vices she allowed herself.

The phone back on its cradle, Sara sat on the bed and thought about what to do with herself. She had never been away from home alone. Even the idea of being away outside the summer seemed foreign to her. But this was the season of college tours. Of half-day car trips with her face jostling against the glass and ice cream socials on quadrangles ringed with freshly planted tulips. She visited colleges named for pioneering suffragettes, for Revolutionary War heroes, for Great Awakening preachers whose portraits, dour and disapproving, hung in reconverted plantation houses. She rode in golf carts and spoke with sophomore representatives whose lives had blossomed into gardens of creative entrenchment. The motifs of these places were all the same, she noticed, the old and the new, ivy choked brick facades and soaring silver buildings with cafes and modernist art in the lobbies.

She tried to play the situation casually, letting the letters from colleges build in a noticeable pile by her bed. But there was something about New York that intrigued her. She had spent sixteen years in Virginia, far enough west that she felt self-conscious about it, where cities were like clumps of loose buildings that had been swept together with a broom. She had driven with friends to Lynchburg and Richmond and felt like she'd been tricked, that her life so far had been slumming in the minor leagues.

She didn't know much about New York, at least not about schools. She knew NYU but didn't like the name, the density of its acronym. The other familiar name was Columbia, which she had a certain feeling about, a suggestion of something wispy and insubstantial that she may have picked up during childhood. Her parents both disapproved. Her mother thought it was too far from home; her father didn't like the neighborhood. They were separated, which gave them more opportunity to press on her from either side.

To start, she mentioned the school and then mentioned it again, later relating to her father that her mother had said something about it, which set things in motion. The visit was to appease her, to remind her that her parents were loving, caring individuals who had her best interests in mind. Then when she settled for something closer to home there would be no hard feelings. She came by train and found out from the concierge, a man with a broad face and cracked, red knuckles, that her father would not be joining her.

She thought about the call she had promised her mother before bed and went back down to the lobby. It was after ten and by now few people were around, one man reading a newspaper and a woman with three suit-cases browsing her cell phone, the screen pressed close to her face. The luggage carts were quiet, herded into a corner, and it seemed that the boys who stood in the lobby, who collected the luggage and looked eager for tips, had gone home. She went back to the elevator, stopping on the third floor this time. It was the same as her own. The carpet had more stains, a cigar burn the size of the quarter just as you stepped from the elevator, and there was a red Lifesaver stuck to the drawer of the lamp stand at the end of the hall. Otherwise it was identical.

Back downstairs, she stood by the automatic entrance with her ciga-rette, playing a quiet game with the door, testing how close she could get it to come to her pinkie toe. Her shoe was off and sat tipped over in the corner while her foot, small and curious, scraped the edges of the cement. The city outside was unfathomable, repressively huge, so much so that looking out she really saw nothing, only the edges of things, the bottom halves of tall buildings and the brake lights of passing cabs.

There was something about the night that made her uneasy. Not afraid, of course, but uncomfortable in a shaky way, like a graveyard, like being in a swamp where you were sure you would step in something. It was a fear she could not understand. The night was something she was sure that she should like. She liked thunderstorms, horse skulls, and the published diaries of serial killers. She liked caves and abandoned houses. But the night was different, for some reason, and she found that near midnight she would begin to feel nervous, glancing uneasily at the thick dark that covered her backyard.

It was childish, but she had a book that she would read when she felt like this. It was called *While You're Asleep. . .* the ellipses fluffy and bold, growing in size to form clouds which held the drawings of the things that went on while this was happening. Her sleeping, that is. It was a book from childhood, not hers, although she wished it were, something she had found in a cardboard box at a garage sale and bought with a handful of spare change. The book had pictures of electrical workers and night watchmen, men in hardhats with serious faces and lanterns above their heads. In anonymous warrens inside of government facilities. On ships. Deep below the surface of the earth. It was a study in brown and blue, comforting shades of orange, each page with two lines of verse and the last, full color and magnificent, of a beaming, contented moon that she had hung on her wall. *At night while you're asleep in bed*, the first lines read, *they keep the world moving instead.*

She noticed from the reflection in the glass that someone was watching her. A boy, young-looking, wearing pale blue jeans and an old bellhop's jacket. He stood in the lobby and stared. She wondered if he was homeless.

"You can't smoke inside," he said, through the glass, when he saw her watching. He was wide-eyed, messy, with curly hair that clung to the tops of his ears.

"I'm not," she said, confused.

He responded with something that she couldn't hear. Embarrassed, she turned away, pushing her shoe back on with her foot and looking both ways down the block.

"Sorry," he said, appearing by her side. They stood next to each other for a moment before he turned quickly and held out his hand. She almost jumped from the suddenness of his movement, taking two steps backward before sticking out her own. He began to pull his back but reversed and caught hers as it receded. He held it for a few seconds too long, not even shaking. "I'm Davey," he said, and she found herself stunned, almost, at the insistent anachronisity of such a name, "I work here. Sometimes."

She shrugged. He continued looking down at her hand, like it was something he was required to memorize.

"What I mean is, it sucks, huh?"

"What does?" she asked.

"The smoking. How you can't smoke inside."

"I don't know, what's the difference? Why are you wearing that?" She asked, pointing at the jacket.

"I like it," he said, "it makes me feel like I'm in a marching band."

"You look ridiculous."

She was surprised by her boldness but felt like here, in a city she knew nothing about with a boy like this, it was appropriate. This was a freeing notion.

"What if I told you that you looked ridiculous?"

"But I don't."

"Maybe I think you do. Maybe that's just how I see it."

"Davey," she said in a patronizing voice, and it felt strange, saying the name of someone she had just met in such a personal way, like they were old friends and she was reminding him of a button he always missed, "you have tassels on your shoulders."

He walked away and she smoked. She smoked three cigarettes and the last tasted not quite finished, unripe in a way that made her think of her ex-boyfriend Clark, who filled out his rolled cigarettes with grass, plucking it from lawns with unnecessary flourish. She bought a bagel down the street but it was chalky and stale and she left the rest in the ashtray. On the street, a homeless man with a beard like steel wool pushed a shopping cart overfilled with soda cans and bottles, loose ones falling off every time the wind blew. This worried her very much. Davey came back after a while and stood there, staring at her from the desk, like this was the way men of his type approached women, stunning them into oblivion.

"I know what you're thinking," he said, slithering his hand up the wall and angling his head to the side. "You're going to ask about the ghosts and the old stories and the secret passageways. You think because I work here I have an in on these things. Well, I do, and so I can be the one to tell you that there's nothing. No one got killed here. Nothing bad has ever happened."

"Nothing?"

"Well, when I say bad, I mean interesting bad. You don't want to hear about the bad things. People die in the rooms but never in ways that you'd hope. You here with your parents?"

"No."

"Well. I bet you feel big."

"I'm bored, mostly," she answered.

"But the city," he said, gesturing with his head to show her where it was.

"What is there to do now?" she said, "at this hour." This was a strained attempt at knowingness; she tried to sound bored as she said it.

"There's a million things. You can just walk around and you'll find something to do in ten minutes, less, there's that much going on. Stand in that bodega on the corner and watch the guy behind the counter, he always falls asleep, right on his stool, he doesn't even care. There's a restaurant called Mi-Chou that serves its food in dinosaur eggs. Fake ones. You crack them open with a fork and find your lo mein inside."

"I'm ok here, I think."

"Well, if you need anything," he said, and winked terribly, his eyelid twitching, "I'm your man."

She thought of her room, with the lights off and her half-unpacked clothing scattered on both beds, the yellow shirt that she was sure she had not packed, and wandered off to the bar. She assumed she was allowed in because earlier she had she seen two children inside, stiffly dressed, like dolls, the boy with a crimson bow tie and the girl wearing plaster-white stockings. They were eating peanuts, sitting with a man who talked into the back of his hand, and she thought of her father, the way he used to take her places and introduce her as his ex-wife.

By now though it was nearly eleven, the lights were low, the bar filled with people she imagined must be traveling salesmen. The walls were covered with old neon signs collected from other bars, or manufactured to look like they had been, shell-bikinied mermaids and winking waiters with cloth napkins on their wrists, drained of their gas, with double arms for animation purposes that now seemed absurd. One of the men threw peanut shells in his drink, one by one, until the liquid began to drip down the sides. She ordered a virgin Pina Colada and then, sure someone was staring at her, inched her way out of the bar, moving quietly from table to table, until she was back in the hall with the drink clutched to her chest. "For the lady," the bartender said when she ordered, "one wowza hold the wow."

Her mother had packed her a list of things to see on her free day. Sitting on the fire stairs with her drink next to her, she took it out of her pocket and examined it. There were warnings appended to each item. The page was dotted with asterisks and sometimes these asterisks had their own asterisks as well. *Take a walk in Central Park* it read, followed by *not at night*. The list noted that the Empire State building was beautiful but the observation deck not worth the price; there were other buildings with better views that you could walk around in for free. It also noted a deli downtown that made unbelievable blintzes, which her mother had warned her earlier was probably no longer there. *Times Square!* the list said, next to *perverts*, underlined three times.

The list mentioned food again and again, with notes about dirty water dogs, borscht, Cantonese dumplings, and the big pretzels you could get anywhere you went, which made her wonder if the only thing to do here was eat. It also reminded her that she'd had nothing since a tuna sandwich at one train station and a cinnamon bun at the other. She remembered reading about a fourth-floor dining room in a booklet in her nightstand. She walked towards it, trying to conceal the drink in the fold of her jacket, but there was no one around anyway, only the suggestion of movement: muffled noises behind doors, an empty room service cart, a suitcase on wheels left unattended by the elevator.

When she finally did see someone, a jowly old man in khakis and a London Philharmonic t-shirt, he seemed flustered, brushing against her as he hurried to the elevator. *On this spot* a sign printed on sepia-toned paper said, *Babe Ruth put his fist through the wall*. Before this was a La Quinta, she assumed.

No one was in the restaurant either. The lights were bright but the tables were empty, place settings untouched and glasses upside down, white-clothed, like furniture in an abandoned house. "Where is everyone?" she wondered, and thought of couples tip-toeing around sleeping children, men in loosened ties perched on the ends of beds, suffering from acid indigestion, griping to tall women slumped on the mattress with their high-heels still on. She began to suspect that the whole city was asleep, and if not asleep, then in bed, with a newspaper, doing the crossword.

Then she noticed Davey, leaning with his elbow on the bar, talking to a kid a little older than himself. He waved and walked over to the table.

"Well," he said, straightening his posture. He looked like an idiot, in his jacket, smiling for no reason.

"Yes," she said, "I came," as if he had asked her to. She had not known that he was allowed to leave the lobby. But here he was. His "well" was one of pleased reaction to a small amount of luck, spoken like a man who finds his child's lost cat at his doorstep.

"Listen," he said, and started to sit down. He realized this breach and pushed the chair back, slowly, returning to his elbow with his face pressed against his hand. "The restaurant closes at quarter past," he almost whispered, "but I'll see if I can pull some strings."

"Why, thank you, Davey," she said sweetly, making a conscious effort this time, putting extra stress on the name. It sounded so stupid that she could not help but repeat it. He raised an eyebrow, trying to look bemused. His brow twitched when he did this and she laughed softly.

While he was gone, she pulled the napkin from its rollers and watched the door to the kitchen. Instead he came out the other way, walking up quietly and poking her in the back of the head.

"Victor is a sack of shit," he said, still standing behind her. "He sweats in everyone's food. But don't worry, not in yours, I talked to him."

"So this means?"

"Did you doubt me? Tonight's special: chicken, in some kind of reduction, pigeon peas, a rice. Wild or yellow, I think. And you get one drink. One, that's it, so choose wisely. Of course, I'm going to assume you're twenty-one."

She could tell he wanted her to turn her head to acknowledge him, so she didn't. She could hear him breathing behind her. The two of them stood, silent, like he had frozen while pushing in her chair.

"Do you usually wait tables in that jacket?" she asked.

"I don't usually wait tables at all. This is just your lucky night."

She ordered a Long Island Iced Tea and it came quickly, browner than she'd imagined, a dented umbrella floating near the top of the drink. The bartender he had been talking to was gone and she suspected he had made it himself. It tasted interesting, hazy and muddled with sharp edges, like something you wouldn't be able to make without a recipe. At home, the things they drank were simpler: pineapple juice and vodka, rum and soda, pinches of liquor stowed inside Gatorade bottles, so weak she spent half the night drinking brightly colored concoctions and the rest peeing them out.

Compared to that, this kind of drinking seemed like a luxury. She decided to make the most of it. When Davey came back with the food she pushed the half-finished drink back toward him. "I don't know about this," she said.

He brought back several more and each she rejected, taking dainty sips with a straw and poking at the ice in the glass. The complaints were specific, untrue, and designed to make him wonder. "Davey this tastes like turpentine," and "Davey, this smells like toilet water," using his name each time, to soften the criticism and make him realize how silly it sounded.

Finally he brought a whiskey, bourbon, in a small glass. In her experience this was something drank by boys with rough edges, the kind who vomited proudly in the beds of other people's pickup trucks. The liquid was murky at the top but toward the bottom turned almost yellow. The ice floated like dead aquarium fish, the taste fiery and bitter but pleasant in a strange autumnal way. What is this like, she thought, and decided on a flaming bag of raked leaves.

Looking down she noticed something else. In the glass were two dead gnats. Small ones, with diaphanous wings, still, like they were floating in amber.

Davey was still there, picking up her dirty dishes. "There's something in this," she said.

"What?"

She wondered if it was unladylike to directly reference what was floating in your drink. He looked at her. She pointed at the glass.

"I don't see anything."

"They're gnats," she answered, "they're dead."

Like before, he made a face where he seemed poised to say something interesting, a confident face, but nothing came out. This was a strange thing about him. He never seemed shy or confused, he made big, sweeping gestures, but then the words fizzled. Or didn't come out. He touched the buttons on the jacket and she could tell by his grin that he enjoyed looking stupid. "This is what happens when a girl tries to drink whiskey," he said.

She went back to her room and lay on the bed, opening the book she had brought to somewhere in the middle. It was by Blake, who her father had called "the best kind of lunatic," and borrowing it she found quickly that she liked the pictures better than the poems. The book had been hers for two years but she had not finished it, never taking it out of her traveling bag. When on vacation she would page through it while she fell asleep. Now she focused on "The Clod and the Pebble," with its penitent looking lambs and bulls. Its springing, happy frogs. This Davey, she thought, he is ridiculous but he is all there is. He is like a pinball machine loaded with grapes.

She realized she was drifting off. How can you think like this, she thought. All there is? You are in the city and the city is full of things. Strange things. Disgusting things. Two hundred million more things than she could ever find in her town, where the one gas station sold everyone their milk.

She thought of the other book, the children's book with its nice drawings, and realized she had found one of these men. The men who work through the night and hold up the sleeping city on their backs. She had met one and he reminded her of her little brother who was thirteen and threw water balloons at the girls he liked. *These men, these men and oh! their jobs*, it read, *they fix the pipes and washer knobs.*

It was eleven by now and she called her mother, dialing on her back with the receiver on her chest.

"Bored. Tired. The TV doesn't work," she lied.

"I hope your father feels guilty for this. Leaving you alone in a city. I don't care about snow, it's shameful."

"Mother there's a boy here. He's ugly and boring but he's proposed and I think I'll say yes."

"Sara, it's too late for this."

"He asked for my virginity. Ten dollars, I said. Ten dollars and an ice cream sundae."

"I hope when you are my age you are blessed with a child as horrible as yourself."

"Oh mom," she said "I haven't even been outside. I stayed in here all night, being safe. I'm sure the muggers are getting desperate."

"Don't say it like that's what I wanted. I want you to enjoy yourself."

"Oh well. There's tomorrow."

"Have a good time honey, please."

"I will. I'll be home soon and we'll have a talk about disappointment."

"See everything you want to see."

"I will mom. Goodnight."

"And please, make sure your door is locked."

But now that she was awake, sleeping seemed like the last thing to do. She was alone, in a city, and she did not know when she would be back. She was an adult. She could stay up all night and watch the sun rise in a park. She could do, within reason, anything she wanted.

Outside the hotel, steam leaked from manhole covers. The lights were on in the closed Walgreens across the street; a man was doing something far back in the aisles and she could see the top of his head as he paced back and forth. Cabs came, one after another. She watched the people get out. Men in beige trench coats, people with their hands in each others pockets, kids with suitcases who walked with their heads toward the sky. A woman caught her shoe on the lip of the storm drain and cursed loudly as it fell off, getting to her knees on the wet ground and looking down the hole where it had gone.

"I've smoked thirteen cigarettes," Davey said, lighting up another as the door opened. She knew that he would come. "My lungs are seething."

He offered her a cigarette. She took it and put it in her pack. "Is that a record?" she asked.

He thought for a second. "I have a ton of bad habits. I eat jellybeans like they're actual beans."

"That many?"

"Like they're cereal," he said.

Never had she met a boy like this. His incompetence was stunning, fearless in a way that seemed almost accidental. Boys who were dumb were usually attractive. If they weren't, they tended to keep their mouths shut. She looked at his face for a long time, at his messy start to a beard and his thin, solid nose. His eyes were the color of mud puddles.

"Davey why don't you show me something," she asked, pretending to yawn.

"You don't listen, do you," he said. But already he was moving, stubbing out his cigarette, and reaching to grab her arm. She followed. He walked like he'd had something in mind the whole time. Up the stairs in the lobby, Through a corridor. Back to the dining room on the fourth floor. The lights were off now; she walked with her hands out in front of her to keep from striking the tables. He walked through the kitchen, up another staircase, through a darkened hallway with a bare light bulb and a long string. They stood in the small circle of light in front of a steel door. "This is it," he said.

He opened the door and they were standing outside, on gravel with darkness all around them. The lights of the city were gone and she heard a thin whistling that must have been the wind. She could not see where Davey was, and suddenly felt afraid.

"This is the garden," he said from a ways off, "the person who built it may have been insane but I don't know the story. I don't know anything about it. That's why I didn't want to take you here in the first place. But you asked. I do know this: at night it's spooky as hell but during the day it's just ugly."

As her eyes adjusted she saw that the gravel stretched to brick walls that joined together to form a box. There were stone pots and a wooden bench with the slats removed. It was still very dark, and the feel of this place unnerved her.

"It feels like a cave," she said, and sat carefully on the edge of the bench, "I ask for you to show me something and this is where you take me?"

"I warned you. I warned you there was nothing, and you wouldn't listen."

She thought about how it would feel to slam the door and leave him locked outside. She could retrace her footsteps, go back to her room, and go to bed. Davey was still too far off for her to see, in the thick shadows along the brick wall. She listened to the sound of his breathing. It sounded like he had a cold.

As she stood near the door, she noticed there was a spot in the brick where the light shone in. A thin beam of it was cast upon the gravel. There was a hole, the kind of window you would have when imprisoned in a castle turret, she imagined. Through it, the city was a neat box with glowing edges. She walked up to it. The dark windows of office buildings sat across the street like closed eyes. But the box was small and it was hard to see much. Across the street she noticed a crew of construction workers, on the roof, with orange safety vests and hard hats. They were asleep.

She was pressed against the stone, craning her neck, when Davey came up from behind. He rested his hands on her hips. "They do this all the time," he said in her ear, "they make a racket half the night and then they take a nap. I think they're using." There was something unwholesome in this. He moved one arm up to her shoulder and began to turn her, like a piece of furniture.

She thought of the last words of her book, the ones that gave her comfort and made everything seem neatly cyclical. *And as you wake your little head, these tired men go off to bed.*

She thought about her mother. "Think about Harper," she would say, whenever Sara seemed inclined towards some kind of romantic mischief. This was a character on the Wednesday show, the illegitimate heir to a wristwatch fortune with Bernese puppies named Bijoux and CoCo Chanel. But this was different. Davey was nothing like the boys in that show, who were either bland and well-intentioned or quietly conniving. He seemed to have the worst qualities of both.

But there was a breeze in the air, the faint smell of exhaust, and the sound of people in the streets. He pressed his lips against hers, and while this was not something she wanted, she found it barely unpleasant all the same, like a bad movie with beautiful scenery. He tightened his grip and nudged her against the wall. His breath did, after all, smell like jellybeans, red ones, the spice kind that hinted of clover. The night buzzed with cold electricity, a mist in the air, and a billboard flashing in the corner of her eye. Davey put his hand on her stomach. "Oh baby baby baby," he said, "you have the sweetest little mouth." ❧

Will of the Stunt Double

Eric Morris

Let me be remembered a headhunter,
a drama queen, a love-struck stalker.
Anything feigned when I had the chance.
I hereby leave, halfhearted, in my stay:
a fire retardant flak jacket, a limited edition
B-side movie reel. Like I, they have decreased
in value. I have nothing less to offer
than my role as a snake charmer on daytime TV.
I bequeath to whosoever, a photo album
from my stint of driving a high-performance
Mercedes off cliffs with bloodlust and bravado.
For my daughter, Mercedes, who time let unlove me,
my army fatigues from a valorless HBO war
that went straight to video without a sequel.
Is sympathy demanded from onlookers,
the countless takes not stricken from record?
Viewer, did I leave tricks unturned?
A cartwheel through a pit of crocodiles?
A belly dance with a necklace of razorblades?
A controlled, live-action sequence burn
in *Escape from Alcatraz* (the unedited version)?
My heroics, spliced together, go unremembered,
cancelled after the low-rated second episode.
My trapdoor is never just a stage prop.
My rehearsal a lifetime without spotlights.
A lifespan rumored to have stage fright.
The will to disappoint. I will disappoint when fired
from a cannon across the Grand Canyon.
There will be no encore unless you forgive me.

Once a Boy

Eric Morris

Once a boy knew how to tie
      his extremities in a half-Windsor.
Warp a human frame with no need

for an emergency blanket, the half-
      moon of a tortoise shell. Too many
limbs to account for, like the steel ribs

of the imploded replica Eiffel tower.
      The supercell made a contortionist
of the skeleton, obscured a line of sight

from the Shoney's to the cut-rate blood
      bank we all came to love so well.
That sudden blindness in the stead

of wanting to be violated just a little.
      Still, congratulations were in order:
to the heavens for making the world

bone cold with all their omniscient
      presence. Once a boy understood how
to resemble a gun swollen in a pocket,

a rabbit's foot pressed into the palm
      of someone else's hand, a thumb tack
lodged in a foot spreading tetanus.

To the echo-friendly hallways of the vacant
      grammar school. How the years filled
with herds of faceless children huddled

in a near three-point stance, no longer
        waiting to kiss their mothers at night.
To the obsolete phone book parted open,

all the yellow pages spread like coffeed
        teeth. Tornado alley left this burnt prairie
like a barren bowling alley with the pins

strewn as if rooks glistening the board.
        Once a boy learned the hard way
that no meant no. Unless there was reason

to believe none of the lawn flamingos
        would be standing come daybreak.
All that pink scattered like a piñata's

entrails, abandoned naked and vulnerable.
        Once a boy went coma-silent when
the western hemisphere buttoned up its

floral blouse and left the world to wonder.
        A place incomplete, the lack of public
baths, altars for sacrifice. A creature left

wanting, like a collie with three legs
        and a deflated basketball. A person who
knew better. Once a boy before

the elements made dents. The need for
        more than a subtle hint. A boy could almost
remember what left him here in the first place.

"I trumpet *Post Road* not out of kindness but out of the purely selfish pleasure I take in a frisky, alert, indepedent magazine whose words and images spring off the page and sometimes turn a somersault or two before they stick their landings in my brain. I also admire the magazine's artistic promiscuity in embracing whatever's good wherever it comes from however it works and whomever it's by."

WALTER KIRN

1 YEAR: $18, 2 YEARS: $34   WWW.POSTROADMAG.COM

Shining Examples of Literary Bastards

Natalie Danford

Novellas, with their not-quite-a-novel-but-too-many-words-to-be-a-story length are the bastard children of the literary world. While the short story requires precision (which makes it puzzling that it's so often recommended to beginning writers as a place to start) and the novel is almost too forgiving (all that opportunity for rambling), like the bed that Goldilocks ultimately selects, the novella is just right. Yet because publishers often don't know how to handle novellas (Pair them with short stories? Pass them off as brief stand-alone books?), they are fewer and farther between than their legitimate siblings. Maybe that scarcity is what makes a well-wrought novella so satisfying.

And when it comes to well-wrought novellas, look no further than the work of Jane Smiley. I wavered about using this opportunity to recommend Jane Smiley's novellas, or really any of her work. Shouldn't I be touting some obscure, long-dead writer waiting to be rediscovered? You already know Jane Smiley's name, have read some or all of her work, and possibly you love it. She's a great writer, no doubt about it, and she has the awards and accolades to prove it. Yet I admire her not for her greatness, but because sometimes she sucks. More than any writer working today, Smiley always sticks her neck out and tries something new—mystery, non-fiction, academic satire, a rewrite of a classic. Some forms she masters, and others she fumbles. The novella, she masters.

The two novellas in Smiley's *Ordinary Love & Good Will* (the title of the book cleverly combines the titles of the two novellas) don't intersect in prosaic ways—no character from one makes a cameo appearance in the other—but they do share a sensibility, an openness to exploring the very definitions of love and family. Smiley's novella "The Age of Grief" (bundled with some short stories in a book of the same title) is equally evocative and so full of inchoate longing (which snaps into focus at the perfect point) that just thinking about it makes my throat close up.

Mary Gordon is no slouch in the novella department either. Her *The Rest of Life* collects three novellas. All three are good, but it's the title novella that haunts me. It follows a woman in the later years of her life who travels back to the scene-of-her-crime in Turin, Italy, where as a teenager she backed out of a suicide pact, something she has never confessed to her family in the United States. She's traveling with her son and his fiancée, and her anticipatory discomfort as the train pulls closer to Turin is excruciating. The novella is the perfect form for this story—any longer and it would feel painfully dragged out; any shorter and the discomfort would lose its power.

Gordon's and Smiley's works date back a while, but Josh Weil's *The New Valley*, consisting of three novellas set in an isolated area along the border between Virginia and West Virginia, was published last year and gives me hope for the future of the novella. All three selections are powerful, but the third, "Sarverville Remains," is the most original. It takes the form of a long letter from a mentally disabled man to the ex-husband of the woman he believes he loves. (When he first spots his dream girl she's giving blow jobs to high school boys in a parking lot.) This novella is both a comedy and a tragedy, and the moments when it swings between those two extremes are heart-breaking. Like the novella form itself, it finds staggering impact in the middle ground. ❧

Alamo Nights

Sumanth Prabhaker

What happened was, I remembered a TV movie I'd seen when I was little, right in the middle of everything. I didn't say anything at the time, with all the yelling and screaming, the strange kinds of bleeding to attend to, because who would stop and listen, at a time like that, all of that happening? Most of the others, when I talk to them, they won't say what TV show they had in their head while it was happening, or how God was speaking to them. I don't talk to them much anymore, anyway. We tried, at first, exchanged phone numbers and emails, even the ones who weren't able to write by then, who had to dictate and have others write for them, due to finger injuries from reaching out too far. And we called each other a few times afterward, but they were quiet phone calls, a little awkward, and there wouldn't be very much emotion when one end spoke up. Most often we just talked about how now there's a Super WalMart there instead. Or maybe it was more emotion than I'm used to.

I want to make clear that I wasn't one of those kids with eight hours every day in front of the TV. I played, or I read books. I'm not saying that's better, that's not my place to say, but what I am saying is, this remembering a TV movie and thinking so hard about it that I forgot momentarily where I was, despite all the yelling and everyone grabbing at me, that was not a thing I could have predicted. It did not fit my character. I know people who are like that. I have friends who, when they heard about the New York bombings, they said it was just like in a movie. They never say if they were thinking of one scene from one movie, or if they meant it just as a thing to say.

And see, this is where, on my arm, I can't bend it anymore. It doesn't hurt, but I just get stuck when I try. I have to use my left hand to eat when I eat, or use a very long fork. They sell extended forks in a mail order catalog I have somewhere around here.

One guy was an actor in the movies. I don't remember his name, he wasn't very popular back then, but now he's in a lot of the famous movies and his picture is on the sides of the CTA buses. There were photographers waiting outside when I showed up, and they asked me if I knew him, if I'd ever seen him snort cocaine. They called it coke.

At the time I was a pastor. I've since given up this position and am now working as a chaplain at a hospital. This was a very difficult decision for me to make, after twelve years of being with my church, but my feeling was, the memory of that TV show was a sign. Have you ever received a sign from God? I believe they come when your life is about to change in a major way, or is at least in need of major change. So I prayed for Jesus to tell me what he wanted me to do, how he wanted my life to change, and Jesus said, Leave your church, Hank, you have other callings. That is when I decided to leave my church. And my new job came to me soon after that, though it was actually two months, and I had to work temporarily at Sears, but two months is very quick for Jesus, who is known to bide his time before opening doors for his children. And the door that was opened for me was, I became chaplain of Northwestern University Hospital in Chicago. Now my job is to pray with inpatients for safe and speedy recovery, especially the ones who come to me rather than my going to them, which I often do. I often go to the section of the hospital where the victims of third-degree burns are placed, and I tell them, take it from me, pain is pain, it hurts and then it leaves, but the matters of the spirit are everlasting. They are by and large a receptive group of listeners.

I knew most of the other people who showed up. One was a girl everyone used to call a slut, and now she had a husband and a daughter, and socks to cover up her tattoos. One was a guy named Jacob, who always carried a calculator with him, and it was no surprise to any of us when we discovered that he was a customer support technician for a computer company. I found all of this to be very nostalgic. There was the old gym, and there was the classroom I led intramural Bible study in, and there was the back entrance to the old gym. Every few seconds someone would sigh or shout that they recognized something, and when we walked past the vending machine, Jacob asked me if we thought it was still stocked with the same bags of Hot Fries, and everyone shared a good laugh.

Most of us are thirty-three or thirty-four by now, so that makes it different. Most of the group was married, I found out, and the ones who weren't kept their hands in their pockets the whole time. I wasn't married at the time. I had tried the internet for a while, but it was an anxious period for me, always wondering, how do I know I'm chatting with who I think I'm chatting with? How do I know it's not actually a man in disguise? I'm not saying I hold anything against them, the men who like other men, they are children of God just as we all are, and without the blood of Jesus how different am I, but my feeling was, find your own internet dating site for once instead of crashing mine, which is reserved for Christians of the Baptist denomination, not gays or those like them, whom I am sure have their own personal dating website. That is why it is called baptistcourtship.com and not something else. And I was matched with a woman named Patricia, and we fellowshipped in the monitored chat rooms for a few months, but when she asked if I thought we were finally able to trust each other enough to exchange pictures, I prayed about the status of our relationship for a long time, and I said, Jesus, if this is what you want, for me to be with Patricia, then don't hesitate to let me know, and I looked down just then and saw the spot on my knee where

Helen's fingernail had caught and given me a small cut so long ago, and I immediately cancelled my subscription, thinking, Thank you, Jesus, for giving me an answer, as much as I dislike being alone.

And Helen was there, too. And she was stunning. She waved at me through the window in the door, and I waved back, and it was very much like fifteen years ago, and I felt as nervous as I had back then, the same feeling of being punched in the stomach by numerous fists, and then two little girls walked in ahead of her. I almost turned to leave right then, but I told myself, Keep your cool, Hank, anything is possible, perhaps they are someone else's children. And then Helen walked in looking more pregnant than any pregnant person I'd ever seen, so I went up to her and said, I would like very much to hug you, Helen, but I'd better not, and she laughed and patted me on the shoulder and said, Hank, it has been too long.

See and this is where I have to do this kind of high-five thing from the side instead of shake hands, because of all the nerve damage to my fingers.

And I am not someone who looks at internet pornography, though I feel compassion and understanding towards the men who do. But I do not struggle with pornography like other men, I have learned to suppress my desires by slapping myself in the face whenever unclean thoughts come to me, and when that doesn't work I stretch a rubber band out and snap it on my thigh, and if that doesn't stop me from entertaining my depravity then I will stretch out the rubber band again, only this time I will aim it directly at my organs, and by that point I will be in too much pain to objectify God's creations, and that is what keeps me from looking at the internet or flipping through my old high school yearbook with lust in my heart like other men. I did not have her in mind when I filled out the RSVP. The idea only came to me just when I arrived.

When we dated, I was much thinner than the way you see me now. I had more hair on my head. Also I had less hair on my shoulders, though I wore a shirt that covered up all the way to my neck, which I bought new, just for the occasion. But what I am saying is, she is stunning and pregnant and I am less thin and more bald and hairy-shouldered and I am thinking, how could I have thought would happen what I thought might happen?

But there is a thing you learn in Seminary, and that is, keep your cool, no matter what happens, and if you get scared, pretend like you're keeping cool anyway. So I kept my cool and said, How far along are you, and she said, Twelve months. And I didn't think that was possible, but she just shrugged and said, Neither did I. She looked sad, saying that, but I've been told there are certain psychological consequences of being pregnant, such as mood swings, so I kept quiet about it and said, I would like to meet your husband, and she said, Hank, I'm not married, it's just me and the kids.

And boy, did that change things.

I do not think it was a very famous movie. It was in black and white, on one of the classic movie channels. I was very little when I watched it. Our babysitter then was our next-door neighbor, Jenny, but as soon as our parents left she would call her boyfriend over and they would go up to our parents' bedroom and shut the door. My brother was old enough that he could read in his room by himself and listen to Jennifer and her boyfriend through the wall, but I had to stay downstairs and watch television.

There were many other women in attendance at the reunion, but there is a reason that Helen was more important to me. And that reason is, she was the one who loved me back.

And it has been fifteen years since then, and now here is someone who knows what my underpants look like, who actually has one pair of underpants I gave her one night, here with her pretty twin daughters and no husband, and I am one who believes in divine intervention. I know Jesus. I have known him since I prayed the prayer and invited him into my heart at age six, and I am well acquainted with his personality. And Jesus is the kind of God who, sometimes he looks down at his creation and sees one of his children in misery, not quite misery, but not at his best, alone and without anyone to keep company, still with the friendship bracelet his girlfriend gave him so long ago, tied around his bedroom doorknob, and Jesus says, Enough is enough, Hank, some people, they've just had it far too hard, and guess what, you're one of those people. And he arranges everything better than I could ever have imagined, and my job is only to say, Thank you, Jesus, for being so understanding, and walk right over to Helen and tell her everything Jesus wants me to tell her, though at first maybe not in front of her children.

So later on, we were all sitting in the auditorium, and the movie star was up on stage, finishing his speech, and it was actually a very inspiring message he had to say. Even now I remember a lot of what he said. Here before you is an example of a true rags to riches story, a true American success story that began right here, in this very room, in these very seats that you people are occupying. Everyone was standing and clapping, and that was when I put my hand on Helen's back. And that felt good, to be near her like that. It was like being on fire, much better than that.

This is how far I can lift my arm now. It's difficult, because people wave hello, and all I can do is nod my head up and down like I'm listening to music.

The movie was called *Alamo Nights*. It was a war movie, in black and white. It was about three Mexican soldiers, but one of the soldiers had a fake mustache, and there were a few scenes where it was falling off. I don't think they were Mexican in real life. I hadn't yet remembered all of this at the auditorium, though, it only came to me later.

The movie star was saying, I look at all the people here, all the beautiful many-hued eyes, all the clean teeth, and I wonder if really, deep down where my soul is, if I haven't strayed too far from this magic place. If really I was born here, and will remain here until the day I die. Then he looked up at the ceiling and lifted both arms, which is the pose he makes on the posters for all of his movies. I remember all of this with clarity.

And by then Helen was crying, due to its being such an emotional speech, and I was moving my hand across her back in slow, soothing motions to show her that I still cared for her and felt deeply about her, especially when she was crying, especially knowing all the mood swings that come from being pregnant, and I would still be there for her even if she never called me back after we went to her grandparents' lake house and did all those things I never thought would happen to me. And her girls were crying as well, due to the actor's references to the emotional scenes in his more famous movies, and I leaned over to touch their backs as well, but they didn't seem to notice, because they were crying so hard.

After that it was time for dinner.

And dinner was okay at first. Helen and Jacob walked out of the auditorium with me, and in the hallway there was a circle of people from our class, including my old friend Jonathan, and this minor league baseball player, and a woman who had attended my church for a few years, and the movie actor, and a few people who snuck in to take pictures of him, and when they saw us, they pulled me into the middle of the circle and said, Hank, what perfect timing, we were just in the middle of deciding who could take care of the kids while we eat dinner, there are more than a few of us who had no time to find babysitters, and the alumni coordinator said that was our responsibility, and we thought at the exact same moment, Hank is a strong, Christian man, he would never allow our children to be hurt, why not give him this chance to shine, right here at our fifteen-year reunion. And I looked at Helen, hoping to see her shake her head no, but she must have been caught off guard by another mood swing, because she said nothing. And though I wanted very much to sit next to her and make slow, soothing motions across her back while eating dinner, there is another thing you learn in Seminary, which is, a pastor is always on duty, though duties should not be performed just to win someone's heart.

So they gave me a bag dinner and a plastic spoon, and I led a few of the children down to the gym where the others were.

The plot of the movie went like this: first there is a group of three Mexican soldiers, and they are running away because they stole a brick of gold from an American military base. This was the general's idea, and the other two soldiers are just helping him out. There is very little talking during the movie.

I will say that I felt more than a little left out, eating my hamburger, when through the vents I could hear everyone else talking about champagne, but I knew God had given me this task, and I knew it was a very important one. Was I about to shirk my responsibilities and leave these children unattended to pursue a crush? A crush from fifteen years ago? I was not. I watched those kids harder than anyone had ever watched them. I saw it when a boy took his pants off so he could sit on another boy's face and fart. I saw a little girl climb to the top of the bleachers and try to jump off, and I caught her before she jumped. I talked to Helen's daughters while they sat in a corner and wrote their names in the air with their fingers, Audrey, Blanche, which was very harmless compared to jumping and farting, but I watched them anyway. They were beautiful.

This is how it makes my nose twitch when I try to make a fist. See how it twitches?

The American soldiers chase after them, but pretty soon the Mexican soldiers believe they have gotten away, in their desert hideout, which is an abandoned house that they believe is too hot and without water for the American soldiers to get to. They kill a deer and cook it over a campfire, and then they spend the night telling stories to each other. The general's story is about his wife and kids, and how they eat burritos with hay stuffed inside because they are so poor. He says he needs this gold brick to live. The two soldiers are whittling around the fire, nodding their heads.

Seeing Audrey and Blanche play together so quietly, it gave me an idea, which was, if I found Helen by the time the reunion dinner was over and everyone dropped off their kids at the hotel and changed clothes to go to the late-night reunion party at the Brando Memorial Dancehall, which the movie actor had been kind enough to reserve for us, we could tell each other all the things that had happened since the night after the prom, like college, like jobs, and the time I was almost hit by a car, and I could explain the ways my theology has changed, and that I would be a good match for her if she would only let me, that I think children are the most important thing in the world.

And I started to talk to Audrey and Blanche, and they said that they were adopted, that they played piano, that Chopin was their favorite. I learned that Helen worked as a caretaker at a museum, and they often joined her in giving tours of the museum, when they had the day off from school.

And I thought, what a perfect life for Helen, almost perfect.

The movie ends with the three Mexicans hiding in their desert house, and in the background is the sound of footsteps. And the general says, Oh geez, it's the Americans, they've found us. And the other two soldiers shrug. The footsteps get closer. This was all my idea, the general says, I have endangered the lives of two good soldiers, how stupid of me, just for a brick of gold, we all will die and I will be responsible for your deaths. And the footsteps get even closer. And the soldiers nod their heads. The brick of gold is in front of them, on a log. And then the general says something that I found to be deeply sad, even at the age of four or five. He says, I regret doing what I have done. And he walks to another room, and after a long pause, there is a sound of a gunshot, and a sound of falling, and the two soldiers don't even flinch.

And by this point all the children were screaming, and when I looked up I saw something strange, which was, the left side of the gym was on fire. I found out later that it was the movie actor's son who had done it, with a lot of twigs and a pile of gym shorts and some lighter fluid, but I didn't know that at the time. He looked as scared as the other kids. I started shouting for everyone to crowd in the center of the gym, where the fire was farthest away. How many children were there? I couldn't tell you. I cannot to this day tell you. All the doors were blocked by the fire, which was growing into a circle around us, and already two or three of the kids had tried to jump over it to get out, and I couldn't see if they made it, but their screaming was the loudest now, and it was also with a funny gurgling sound, which only made the rest of the kids start crying even more, and there was one boy sitting on top of the basketball hoop, and he wouldn't climb down, but he was choking from all the hot air and smoke, and he kept making the universal choking signal, which is to wrap your fingers around your neck like this, and I kept shouting for him to climb down, and finally he got too dizzy from all the smoke and he fell. There was a sound when he hit the floor.

And that is an awful thing, to see a child die. It is the worst thing you could ever see.

All the flags from sports tournaments started to catch after that, and it looked like the entire wall was on fire. Some of the flags fell, and all the pieces of hot ash got on our skin and in our eyes, so we had to run to the other end of the gym, but the bleachers were starting to catch, so we had to backtrack. By then the parents had left their dinners to come stand near the doors and shout for their kids, which was not very helpful, due to when the children heard their parents, many of them ran straight through the fire, and after that the parents would scream and cry for a long time, and pretty soon the parents stopped calling for their kids at all, even when the kids were calling for them.

And that was when I decided that if there was no exit, then it was my job to make an exit. So I took a chair and set it just before the fire, which had grown taller than me, and all the kids lined up behind me. My plan was for each of us to step on the chair and jump over the fire and then run out the gym doors. And I put Audrey on the chair first, but she was too scared to jump, and so was Blanche. No one would jump. I said, we have to jump, there is no other way, but no one would jump. And my feeling was, someone had to jump, at least to test the plan out, and the person to test it should be me. That way, if it were too high, I would be the only one to die, and they could stay safe in the middle of the gym for a few more minutes.

So I got on the chair and jumped over the fire.

And when I did finally land, some people came over and patted my arm with their coats and sweaters, and I ran to the doors and said, Kids, do like I did, step on the chair and jump over, but the kids said that the chair had caught fire, too, and now the fire was too high for them to jump over.

And then I saw Helen, and she was crying, and I tried to put my hand on her back to make slow soothing motions, but it hurt too much to lift my arm. And then I thought again about the general and his two soldiers, sitting in that tiny desert house, eating the deer they'd shot. I thought about the brick of gold, and burritos stuffed with hay. A man came up to me and grabbed my shoulder. He asked me what happened, if I saw. He asked if I saw his boys. The footsteps keep coming closer. The general looks out the window, to see how far the American soldiers are. The man grabbed my neck and punched me. They are coming closer. He covers up the brick of gold with deerskin and looks at his two loyal soldiers. And he speaks. He says, I regret doing what I have done. Then he leaves, and there is a sound of shooting, and a sound of falling, and the footsteps coming closer, and a bugle noise that sounds very authentic and Mexican, and then silence.

And this is what Jesus was telling me with this memory. Do not be like that general. Do not regret doing what you have done, which is to stand by and do nothing to help those children.

And all the parents were calling the fire department or throwing water from the drinking fountain, and the fire kept growing larger and the heat kept pushing us back farther, and I thought, there is nothing we can do within our power.

And I knew I had to do something, so I will tell you what I did. I prayed for them. I prayed every prayer I could remember, the Lord's prayer and the 23rd Psalm and the famous prayers of Martin Luther King, Jr., and when I couldn't think of any more I started making up my own prayers, for safety and for deliverance, and for the blood of Christ to put out what needed putting out. In the middle of everything I prayed. And when finally I had run out of words and I opened my eyes to look inside the gym, peering through the parents and through the flames, I saw an angel come down, dressed in a white robe that was brighter than any fire, and I saw him open his arms to embrace all the children. ❧

Victor LaValle's BIG MACHINE

Laura van den Berg

Victor LaValle's *Big Machine* was an impulse buy at the bookstore. I had just finished a day's work on my own book-in-progress and was wandering the shelves aimlessly, looking for I-didn't-know-what, my reading mood at once particular and inexpressible. I picked up and set aside book after book, unsatisfied. That is, until I came across *Big Machine*. As it would turn out, LaValle's latest novel was precisely what I was in the mood for. While I'd been hearing about LaValle, and *Big Machine* in particular, for a while I'd never read his work, but a jacket copy touting a suicide cult survivor, mysterious letters, and "a band of paranormal investigators comprised of former addicts and petty criminals, all of whom had at some point in their wasted lives heard what may have been the voice of God" hooked me immediately (how could it not?)—and also left me wondering how LaValle would manage to pull all this off.

From the first page, I fell happily under the spell of the novel's protagonist, Ricky Rice, and soon I was deep in the world of janitorial duties at Union Station in Utica, New York, and secret orders in the Northeast Kingdom of Vermont, and haunted pasts, deep in the loopy and sad world of *Big Machine*. Ricky Rice is a deliciously layered protagonist, his voice at once generous, cutting, funny, and painful, and this is a novel of big ideas and big heart.

In the novel's opening chapter, Ricky is summoned to the Washburn Library, where he joins a band of misfits that become known as the Unlikely Scholars, all there to do mysterious and possibly crucial work under the shadowy scrutiny of a man they call the dean. In a different kind of novel, LaValle could have spent the entirety of *Big Machine* exploring the complexities and contours of this peculiar compound, but Ricky's story is far more expansive and ambitious; it is a story that compels this reader to offer up one of the highest compliments that can be paid: I've never come across anything quite like it. ❧

Summer Evening, Hopper 1947

Christopher Tozier

Someone is firing rockets
across the water
too far away to hear.
Each named for a flower,
save one for a flock of larks in flight,
one for an emperor-turned-dragon.
The lake greedily collects the sparks
in her dark apron, then walks to the basement.

A young man and woman have turned on a porch light,
erasing the exploding rockets from view.
She refuses a cigarette. He explains
his temper using words neither of them understand.
His hands flare like chrysanthemums.
Someone ignites the fuse and runs.
Someone stands firm,
testing how closely they can withstand
the phosphor of night.

House of the Fog Horn, No. 3, Hopper 1929

Christopher Tozier

Men in overalls regularly enter
through the well-house
yet are never seen leaving.
The small windows are painted black,
the main door padlocked and mute.
What strange mechanics exist there in
the three-foot-thick walls,
what steampunk gyro
powered by centrifugal fission
and perpetual solitude.
Tensile springs and hydraulic pins
inflate a bellows.
The hot furnace burns but its chimney rises
forever into the sky.

From that,
a voice box explodes inside the fog,
telling a story in one stanza
of glacial mercy, the traffic of whales,
a relentless pull toward hardness.
The outbound sailor must follow that voice
but know when close is close enough,
veering east at the last possible moment.
He would do best to ignore the voice behind,
however it is generated or why.

Raw Material

Alanna Schubach

Leah, I'm not writing you this for the reasons you think.

When I'm finished I'll give this to your mother and ask her to pass it on when you're ready, which I don't think will be too long from now—but long enough.

You know I worked in the office of the psychologist at West Hempstead High School, who spent more of his time collecting antique books than he did seeing students. The books were not for reading, it was supposed to be understood. They were the objects that take on mystical heft, things you feel echoing in your chest when you look at them, a pleasant alien thumping from within. The psychologist would look at me as though I had spit on him when I'd take one down, but he couldn't say anything.

One of the books had several photos of 19th century women in the throes of hysteria. Their faces were satanic, with rolling eyes and protruding tongues. They wore white nightshirts and were tangled in bedsheets, their hair loose, their hands uplifted as though toward some invisible master. They grinned like people who had broken through the final membrane of self-consciousness, self-awareness, and had been handed over to a nightmare plane where they could only laugh into the darkness. My mother looked nothing like that.

What she told me much later was that my father had taken her dancing at a club in Manhattan. It was a rare and special event—he usually worked very late. She'd gone to the bathroom and over the rush of her peeing heard two girls gossiping, pausing (she imagined) to purse their lipsticked lips in the mirror.

"Chip's such a good kisser," one said, and the other answered with an agreeable trilling laugh. It floated up to the ceiling and over the stalls, where my mother could see it. Chip being my father, your great-grandfather.

You don't want a Bat Mitzvah, you announced this evening at dinner. You don't want to be formally indoctrinated (your word) into a religion whose members consider themselves the Chosen People. I remember you blanching similarly when you were placed in your elementary school's Gifted Program; you didn't like that word, though you weren't sure why—"gifted."

Bryan was having dinner with us. Your mother won't go so far as to take him in, but he is over more often than not. He was there to back you up before your parents could even react, which I think might have been disappointing to you.

"Nobody's *chosen*," he said. "Nobody's even good."

"Yeah," you said, and I heard the chord of doubt there, vibrating softly underneath the ringing confidence. But soon enough even that will be gone, I think.

Your mother chose to make it a joke. "Great," she said. "I'm surrounded by misanthropes."

"Missin' what?" your father said. "I'm not missin' anything."

The doubt was smothered then by the rage that came into your eyes. You become almost possessed when you sense you are not being taken seriously. It's a strange thing to say, but I hope some distant knowing part of you treasures these moments, when emotions are so pure and clear, because that also goes away.

It's true there are a lot of ways to discredit me. I did used to take the train into Williamsburg, trying to find a Hasid who would give me the recipe for making a golem. I had heard once that there was a recipe in the Book of Creation, but I didn't know where to find the book, nor did I know any mystics who would explain it to me, nor could I read Hebrew. The Hasidim always turned me down, pushed me away (not literally: they can't touch any woman they're not married to), said *Vat is wrong with you?* but not, I think, because no such thing existed, but rather because they thought me a heathen, undeserving. It's also true my first husband put a gun in his mouth, which is a good way, according to everyone I knew at the time, to make a woman go crazy.

My first husband had never grown up in some ways. He was like you in his respect for unadulterated feeling. He once expressed deep disappointment in me for eating a slice of bread in the middle of a fight. But there was no other food in the house, and the fight had interrupted our plans for dinner, and shouting doesn't make hunger go away. But he thought it meant I wasn't taking our shouting seriously, that I wasn't experiencing it on an adequately profound level. I felt then, as he shook his head in disappointment, a laugh bubbling inside me. I've often thought if we could have laughed away our fights, which is much more possible than shouting away hunger, things might have turned out differently. But instead I threw the half-chewed bread at him and said, "There, happy?"

Coming home and finding his brains sliding down the wall didn't make me crazy; it did the opposite: it drained all the mystery from my life that might have otherwise driven people to find me, at the least, a bit odd.

Because I stood there over his slumped body and saw the clotting blood and shards of skull (at first I could not understand that was what they were; my first assumption was that someone had broken in and smashed my coffee mug over his head, killing him, because that was what the shards looked like to me, pieces of my mug) and gray matter and realized that is all there is to any of us; our grotesque solids and the things you can't see but are nonetheless hopelessly concrete, neurons firing and so on, driving us forward, positioning our limbs, our mouths, what comes out of our mouths, in the most unenigmatic way.

But of course that's not all there is.

Cats are nocturnal, did you know? I don't know what difference that makes for a house cat. It's not like they have anything to forage for, or defend themselves against. Maybe they prefer it that way, having a lazy life. Maybe they just think they prefer it. But you see, they're so blank, you could impose anything upon them.

What happened after my mother's discovery of Chip's infidelity is that she went to bed. But not to sleep. Throughout her hysterical paralysis, her eyes were open and unblinking; maybe she did a kind of dreaming, dreams overlaid with the hairline cracks in her bedroom ceiling. We traded shifts squeezing the eye drops the doctor prescribed into her eyes at forty-five second intervals, and then gently wiping the moisture off her flabby cheeks.

Our cabin in Maine is where nothing happened. Not an absence of events; an aggressive *nothing* that would take place every time we went. Nothing echoing off the peaked wood paneled ceilings, the plaid couch, the loft bed, the fireplace made of ancient stones you could imagine men in high boots bending over and pulling out of the quarry, from beneath burning cold clear water. "Maine" was a vague concept; really we felt, while inside the cabin, unmoored from time and place. When we set down our suitcases and closed the front door behind us it was as though the cabin had welcomed us with its long and creaking arms again and I could hear a sucking sound as we detached gummily from the outside. The air would shimmer briefly and we'd be off. We'd be reading beside the fire and then wake up in the loft in a tangle of blankets and arms and legs with a few winking embers in the fireplace below and have no idea how we'd gotten up there, and laugh inside the dark ill-defined world under the covers where it was quiet enough to hear thumping without knowing whose heart it was. My first husband had a very strong heart beat; I could see it jumping under his neck and sometimes at night I'd burrow close so I could feel it pulse against my cheek and think how it meant he'd live for so long. I'd watch for the occasional headlights of a passing car outside to go sliding along the high vaulted ceiling, dispatches from the other world. Of course it was in that world that he pulled the trigger. I was angry for a long time that he'd given me Maine, because to think of it afterwards was so much worse than thinking of slammed doors or thrown bread or how it would look when he would collapse in on himself and I knew the slow unfolding, the extrication to come, the distances we'd have to cross. But even those moments in Maine, in the present tense, were like a sweetness you crush against the roof of your mouth that also burns, to the point of unbearability, not just for itself but for the unfillable hole after the sensation ends.

She forgave him, though. She forgave him even as she lay there locked inside herself. After he died, she kept a bottle of his cologne that she sprayed on her pillow every night. The relatives who would drop by to relieve my father and me of the eye-dropping shifts couldn't know this. Their closed, reproachful faces sent him out of the house. I don't know how much they knew—at the time I was seven and knew nothing myself—but they figured him at fault, the one who had stood behind my mother and pushed her into the husk of her body. The longer it went on, the angrier they became, no longer speaking to him but only making sounds of disgust in his direction that reminded me of oinking. And even to me he became grotesque in his slinking movements. I had a dream of him writhing across my bedroom floor toward me like a huge snake. So my grandparents took me to their house for a while and my father had to hire someone to help with the eye drops, because he couldn't depend on the relatives who hated him. What was strange was that during this separation I worried not about my shamed father nor my frozen mother, but only about Sophie, the cat. We'd had her my whole life and beyond: an old cat needed extra care, and even before the crisis my parents sometimes forgot to leave the door open to the screened-in porch where she could lie in pools of sunlight or hiss futilely at birds through the wire mesh. I'd lie in bed flipping through scenes of Sophie's food bowl left empty, her litterbox overflowing, windows opened in vague awareness of the smell but not of its source, because who, but me, would remember a cat *at a time like this*, Sophie escaping, Sophie turned to red mush in the street, a car speeding away with fur in its tire treads. The psychologist I worked for at West Hempstead High School would have called this *transference*. At least my grandparents thought it was, or they'd just lost enough sleep to my nightly cat-centered wailings, so that soon enough they brought me home.

Leah, could I tell you to stay away from dark-eyed, poetic men? Could I warn you against the belief that it is possible to heal people? I could not.

Bryan is your best friend in the world; you feel you were not known before him, you were a silhouette creeping along the edges of things, impenetrable. But you hadn't realized before him that you felt this way. And now that you know you can't stand the sight of your mother, who was supposed to be the one to understand, who failed you. Apparently I am the matriarch, which makes me picture myself as an oak tree, with people's faces dangling from the ends of my long weathered branches. As such I am expected to offer comfort and wisdom to both of you. But without the benefit of years, of perspective, what I could tell you cannot be heard.

I write this but maybe it's not true. Your mother tries to soothe herself by saying this is a phase. I hate the word as much as you hate *chosen*, since it implies that this is somehow not real life but some other plane to pass through, where nothing should count. And you will pass through it, but not necessarily into something better, or more real.

The golem was to be for my first husband. In the stories a holy man gives life to a creature made of Vltava river mud, who defends the Prague ghetto from riots, fear, invasion—from the outside. I wanted, by proxy, to make the ground shake beneath his feet. Which would then crack and loosen the mold of weariness and self-exhaustion that had coagulated around him, that I couldn't penetrate with my ordinary fists. It's not clear whether I intended his golem to be on the defense or the attack. It wasn't clear, at the time, that my idea had an ancient origin, that it was borne from a childhood backlit by one night in the living room, orange embers in the fireplace, something slinking toward me, the image the one bright pinpoint in blackness. The golem was mute and could be returned to dust. I thought if he could just see what we were capable of—I thought I could literally shake him out of it.

After the suicide, I would take the subway all the way out to the Rockaways, a long ride from where we lived in St. Albans. I let it rock me in its glossy stomach. I passed under the East River twice. I liked thinking about all that water over my head. It was the holidays and as we went through, Manhattan bodies would crowd on and off in their bulky dark coats, paper shopping bags swinging from their wrists. It was hard for me to reject the idea that everyone was mourning the loss of Michael and had just painted a thin gloss over themselves to hide their howling. It's not like you see in the movies, where a haunted person will be slashed with images of whatever disturbing thing they suffered, and they'll violently toss their heads from side to side or make grotesque exaggerated wincing faces to communicate their torment. I'd get off the train and walk along the rocky shoreline, trying to give my body over to the wind's assault, trying not to hunch my shoulders against it, but it was impossible. I still wanted warmth. I still couldn't quite believe in the unbearable tug of nature. Basically, I didn't know what to do with myself. But then my mother got sick, and I did.

When I had nightmares—we called them nightmares, though they also came when I wasn't asleep, dissociated cels from a film strip of twisted, deformed faces—my mother would come into my room with Sophie.

"Cats are half-evil," she said. She didn't have to explain. I'd seen Sophie licking black blood off her talons after killing, because she could. "It's good to have one on your side." Sophie dozed heavily at the foot of my bed, weighted with importance. All children are mystics. In their helplessness, they have no other choice. How many nights did my mother deliver me from horror, singing me from it in her plain voice, infused with an otherworldly beauty that made certain chords vibrate so that I thought my heart might explode? And yet somehow also sent me sinking warmly into the now blank dark behind my eyelids. "Thank you," I muttered once, trying to send her a signal from behind the safe skin of my drifting. I felt her hand moving over my hair, and was certain it would never stop. She spoke as you do only to someone you're sure isn't conscious. "Don't thank me," she was saying. "I'm selfish. I do this for myself." A thread of something strange, something I later recognized as bitterness, wound itself around her voice. "It's so good to be needed."

After two weeks they began to worry about bed sores. She had to be turned regularly, her limbs lifted and moved, soaps and salves applied. I was spared this. My father was the one who cleaned her and changed the sheets with blank-faced determination, as though there was an allotted amount of times to do this before they were even. I think penance may be the opposite of selflessness.

It was clear to me that something had to happen, something more than his entering and leaving the bedroom, his mouth an em-dash in his face. Though I was warned to be gentle, I had tried shaking her. Her body flopped in a boneless way that I barely managed not to scream over. I had thought of denying her the eye drops, but the image of those staring globes drying out and shattering—even if it didn't matter, because she was just, I was trying to accept, going to waste away, something no one needs eyes for—stopped me.

I was sitting in the living room wondering if there was anything that could come next. Years later in my bed that was too wide, in St. Albans, when I couldn't sleep, I'd grow that living room, let it open and spread around me. The parquet floor alone was a world, infinite crisscrossing borders holding in geometric kingdoms. The green couch, before it the glass coffee table and the glass candy bowl on top, hard candies in glossy wrappers whose flavors I could only guess at as I'd sneak one at a time and then try to silently readjust the bowl's contents so my parents wouldn't notice they were less. Although at the time of my mother's paralysis no one noticed, and I consumed half the bowl and even left a multihued constellation of wrappers surrounding it where they remained, unremarked upon, for the duration of her illness. Sophie on the little stone ledge of the fireplace as long as an ember glowed. My father had something he called magic dust that he threw in the fire to make the flames spit purple and blue. I was staring into the dead hearth, its pile of charred flakes, when my mother said my name.

"Coming," I said, before the wrongness struck me. Like how you'll keep flicking the light switch when you know the power's out.

I turned and saw the cat walking toward me from across the room in that loping, singularly bestial way.

"You have to help me," Sophie said in my mother's voice.

"How?" She lifted and licked a front paw, continued acting cat-like in every other way. It was dream logic come to life, how the strangeness didn't occur to me until later, when I was trying to understand why the cat's furled shape on my bed filled me with a kind of humming unease that lay across the passageway to sleep.

"Get me out," Sophie said. "Do it now."

So I dismissed my father and climbed onto the head of the bed and crouched there over my mother, watching her upside-down face until it became a distorted and disturbing right-side-up face, with wide dead eyes drooping toward twin smiling eyebrows. The pupils in the eyes seemed to enlarge and become deep inky pools to dive into. I was waist deep in jet waters. My mother was there skimming her hands meditatively over the surface, her hair suddenly long, trailing behind her on the water in pale swirls. I expected resistance but the water was light as fog as I waded over to her. I took her cold hands as best I could in my small ones. I saw her kiss my father in the rain. I saw her at the kitchen table after I'd gone to sleep, waiting for him, getting haltingly to her feet, thinking she should have something to offer him when he arrived finally from his long day, as though anything she could prepare would be more than herself, which was not enough. Instead she walked upstairs and saw my sleeping face from the doorway, placid as a snake's, unconcerned with loss. She might have been another stray crayon mark on the wall.

"No," I said. She turned to me. Her eyes were like a cat's eyes. "I need you." I felt her hands grip back, and then we were sucked up and out of the water, and we felt the stale quilt under our legs, we were sitting on the bed facing each other still holding hands.

You had your Bat Mitzvah anyway. Afterward you stood in the temple lobby and were unable to swallow a smile of pride from within the circle of praise, but shot through that smile was a beam of awareness that you had given in and were feeling what you were supposed to feel at this pre-appointed rite of passage, that your parents were watching from afar and whispering to each other they had known this would be good for you. You chanted beautifully.

Maybe this does mark the dawning of a consciousness. At the party you and Bryan lurked mostly at the edges of the dance floor, unable to wholeheartedly commit either to the celebration or to the darkness orbiting it. You were not sour but not entirely present. You allowed yourself to be drawn in occasionally but something remained always outside. I'm afraid your life will be harder for your trying to find some way to live. When I look back it seems to me there were only two real moments in my entire life, the rescue and the suicide, two defining poles between which everything else thrums quietly. But now, you: you're also real.

My mother was clearly detaching from what most people call real, but it seemed when she looked at me from her hospital bed she could see empty Rockaway Beach freezing behind me. Shortly before she died she took my hands in hers, which were surprisingly warm. "Thank you," she said, two puffs of air.

"For what?"

With greater force, an actual tone running through the words, she told me, "You know what."

As though she had reached down my throat and pulled out my heart and gripped it dripping before me. I was seized with the memory of the night I removed her from herself: it formed a halo embracing my whole sad life. Because, do you know? I had forgotten the whole thing. ❧

The Politics of Play

Megan Kaminski

My confession: I like playing golf. On late summer afternoons when the day shows its first signs of cooling, my thoughts turn to the golf course. This isn't something I'm proud of. I make up stories to hide my golf activities. Only a few people know about my habit. I plan out my appointments for the week to pick out preferred tee times and cheap greens fees. I lie in bed at night agonizing over my missed par on the seventh hole. Sometimes, late at night, when no one is looking, I even take a club into the backyard and practice my swing.

I'm not your typical golfer. I don't belong to a country club or work in a golf-appropriate profession like business or medicine. There are no business deals to close, no professional or social contacts to impress. While my golf habit isn't something that I would likely bring up with my ecopoetics friends or my Marxist reading group, I wonder if it is something truly worthy of confession. I'm certainly not the only one hiding this secret. During his campaign for president, Obama's camp preferred photo-ops of their candidate playing the more plebian sport of basketball, despite the fact that Obama is also long-time golfer, playing in his adopted home state of Illinois and on Hawaiian vacations. Could a populist president be a public golfer? Or more specifically, is the practice of golf inextricably tied to its function as a marker of social class and conspicuous consumption? Is it possible for golf to be just a game—a system of play that serves an essential function, perhaps just a half-step away from being a basic pleasure like bodily sensations of food and reproduction?

I probably never would have discovered golf if I hadn't moved to Kansas. In Oregon, long hikes in the gorge, or even in Forest Park, occupied a lot of my free time. When I lived in Paris, the Luxembourg Garden was just around the corner. Santa Monica is on the Pacific Ocean. But in the big Midwestern town where I now live, there aren't so many opportunities to easily embrace the outdoors. While moving to Kansas was the catalyst for my interest in golf, strangely enough, my main source of anxiety about my newly chosen sport is generated from the people I come in contact with at the university where I work and the college town where I live. Maybe it's because it still feels odd to be a young woman teaching at a university, or because my own peers often mistake me for a student, forgetting that I am on faculty even after having been introduced to me multiple times in the two years I have been teaching here—whatever the reason, I am probably a little more defensive about my choices than the average person. While most people who condemn my golfing activities are 60s relics who somehow believe that listening to the Grateful Dead and wearing overpriced hemp clothing is equivalent to social activism, I sometimes ask myself if their more cogent objections have some merit. Hugo Chávez has recently labeled golf a bourgeois and wasteful sport, and his objections made me consider the politics of golf more closely. Rather than denouncing the game to mark his tastes—as my colleagues often publicly eschew television and sport as proof that they are interested in "weightier" matters—he proposed using two recently closed courses as sites for public housing, a university, and a children's park. There are housing shortages in Venezuela, and perhaps Chávez is correct to question why Maracay, the site of a government-closed course, has so many slums while the golf course and the grounds of the state-owned Hotel Maracay occupy about seventy-four acres of coveted real estate. While he might not be most Americans' idea of a wholly rational person, I have to wonder if Chávez has a point.

The game of golf certainly carries a lot of baggage. I have a friend, a fellow golf aficionado, who lived in Germany for a year. He readily recalls the cold reception his golf habit received in Berlin. In the middle of a perfectly pleasant bar conversation, golf had the capacity to turn the evening ugly. Apparently, saying you enjoy playing golf in Germany is roughly equivalent to talking about your passionate polo play in the US. It's not so much better in my social circles, and to be honest, my initial ideas about the sport were somewhat in this mode.

Growing up, my interactions with golfers were limited. I lived in Virginia, and the old-school country club about a mile from my house where I imagined that most people played golf still restricted membership from women, Jews, and people of color. None of my parents' friends played golf, and my father discouraged the idea of golf as a sport to me at a very young age, sketching it out as a hobby for dull people of privilege. Perhaps most damning in his eyes, it was a sport where expensive lessons could make up for a lack of athletic ability.

This golf thing has been a recent undertaking. After moving to Kansas two years ago, I found myself with some free time on my hands. My partner has been playing golf since he was a kid, and he thought that going to the driving range might be a fun way to spend an afternoon. I had no intention of picking up golf. I'm in a unique position, perhaps, in thinking that the hobby would hinder, rather than help, my professional connections. I'm a poet, and I don't write the kind of poetry that gives me a cohort of old school dudes, wearing Brooks Brothers clothing and playing lots of golf. Moreover, I had always decried golf as an elitist, environmentally harmful sport. Not only was it irresponsible to play golf, it was decidedly uncool. In my mind, golf was still a hobby for stodgy old guys and their sons, or socially mobile businessmen. While there certainly are golfers with the latest juiced-up drivers, perfectly-planned outfits, and scotch-stocked carts teeing up at their country club, there is also another side to golf.

My first trip to the range was somewhat similar to the first time I went to church. I knew before I got there that my values and general proclivities would separate me from the rest of the attendees, and I considered myself superior to them because of that fact. At the same time, I'm a pretty polite person, and the idea of being inappropriate or embarrassing myself terrified me. So before my first golf outing, I stopped by the discount store to buy a couple of past season Ralph Lauren polo shirts and matched them up with a conservative pair of khaki capris for the big day. At the range, I picked up a bag of balls from the pro shop and joined my friends. I was sure that something would pick me out as an imposter— the way I carried my golf bag, or when my ball nicked the rope marking the limits of the range and hurled it forward a few feet. When I left the house that morning, I had imagined confrontations with snotty golfers related to politics or global warming, but once I was actually there, I was so focused on figuring out how to keep my left arm straight and my head down that I had forgotten my objections to golfing in the first place.

Finally, after about a week of hitting balls, I experienced the perfect uncoiling of my spine on a gorgeous drive. The way my arms felt when the clubface made square contact with the ball. The hollow ping of the driver launching the ball into a whizzing trajectory. Watching that gorgeous curve of flight, the trajectory of the ball through the air. After a few visits to the range, I was hooked. As soon as I arrive at the course, my body awakens—the expanse of sky, the smell of cut grass, and the sound of balls zipping all around me triggers to a different kind of sensation. My mind and muscles simultaneously ready themselves and relax, finding the balance necessary for success on the course. Golf has become part of my life. I welcome the break from my work, from my writing. Breathing in the fresh air, hearing the wind rustle through the trees, and feeling the solidity of a good shot transports me from wherever my brain is stuck, for a few minutes at least.

Playing a round of golf, you can almost picture the original golfers. Just as the scotch imbibed in the golf carts of wealthy golfers had humble beginnings in Scotland, so too did golf. Most people think the first games of golf consisted of shepherds hitting stones around common lands in Scotland while grazing sheep. It's easy to imagine them taking a break to hit stones into rabbit holes. They even had hazards like sand traps, created from sheep seeking shelter from the wind behind bluffs. Golf was originally egalitarian; it was a found game requiring no special equipment or access. And in some ways it is still. While a certain amount of capital is needed for start-up fees like clubs (I bought a great set used for about $150) and greens fees, additional money is no guarantee of pleasure or skill. One of my friends is a scratch golfer, and she plays with the same clubs she used fifteen years ago in high school. She goes to the course wearing an old t-shirt, a sweat-stained hat, and grungy tennis shoes. She's typically the best player on the course on any given day. For her, the pleasure of golf has nothing to do with its social trappings, and the status, good or bad, it connotes.

And there are many different ways to play golf. There are country clubs and expensive accessories, golf clubs that promise to correct any flaw in your game. Each year the golf companies unveil a new selection of titanium drivers with bigger heads and names that are too ridiculous for even a poet to make up—the Sasquatch, the Launcher Ultralite, the Bazooka, the Big Bertha, the XLS Monster, the King Cobra, the Air Force One—and, for the price of purchase, they promise to make any drive go an extra twenty or so yards. But there is also the modest 9-hole course where I play most often. It costs $8 a round on weekday afternoons, and even though the greens aren't kept up to the meticulous standards of the private course down the road, it's pretty nice. There is a little creek that runs through and huge oaks hunker down over the course, providing shade. The groundskeeper keeps the basics well-maintained, but the overall feel between holes is of being in a shady park. There is no bizarre day-glow green grass here. When I pay my fee, there is a plain glass cooler behind the counter: $1 for bottled water, $2 for Miller Lite.

Obviously there is a nastier side to golf—a dirty social and environmental history. For starters, there is the notion of golf as a sport only for rich white men. That country club located near my childhood home in Virginia doesn't do much to break that image. I doubt that they have changed many of their policies. While Tiger Woods has certainly served as a model to open the sport of golf up to people of various races and classes, he still exists primarily in the commercial golf world, where his main task is selling over-priced golf equipment and clothing. There is the environmental impact of unsustainably lush courses in places like Vegas and Dubai, or even country clubs across the country, with their thirsty grass and water hazards that need constant filling. But isn't it still possible to cobble out a space for golf as a sport, something that might fulfill an essential human function?

I'm certainly not advocating a view that operates in some kind of vacuum, removing golf from its historic and cultural contexts because of some intrinsic sense of value, or a misguided sense of purity. Just like, I think, it is important to acknowledge the factory behind the field in your nature poem, it is necessary to acknowledge the problems of golf. However, I'm not sure that those problematic associations are enough to throw out golf all together. In some ways, I wonder if we are quick to discount physical pleasure and play as a valid activity.

I have an acquaintance who flies regularly to locations in the US and abroad to bird watch, what he likes to call "field work." While he has no specific knowledge and makes no contributions to society or science through his "findings"—his personal journal in which he keeps a running tally of bird species that he has observed—he considers this to be virtuous work. Basically, his fieldwork, eco-holiday, or whatever you want to call it, is about the exchange of cash for some kind of cultural capital. He pays money to be able to present a higher tally of observed species when he talks to his bird watching friends. With the environmental impact of the plane ride, consumer goods necessary to be what he considers a proper birdwatcher, etc, the "fieldwork" becomes as problematic as other forms of leisure travel involving the enjoyment of nature, and it is far less honest. Yet, this is certainly a praiseworthy activity in certain social circles, including the town and academic community where I live. While my acquaintance's bird watching practice is at best mildly objectionable, it passes as virtuous due to the positive social associations of bird watching. There is something wonderful about going into your backyard, or out into the parks or fields near your home, and observing birds and appreciating nature. Moreover, there is important work that is done by naturalists in keeping track of bird populations. However, his practice of bird watching bears little resemblance to those virtuous activities.

Last week, on a course near my house, I made my first birdie. Although we were politely attired and had all the proper equipment, my friend and I were probably the only people on the course without golf-specific shoes and the newest drivers. With a father-son duo behind us that looked like they had stepped out of a Patek Philippe advertisement (don't worry, I let them play through on the next hole), I teed up. It was only a par 3, but it was one of the trickiest holes I had played—it was a bit short, but a large water hazard stood between me and the green. Moreover, if I missed the green, my ball would likely tumble into the sand traps on either side, or into the trees behind. Considering the wind and thinking about the hazards, I chose a 5 iron, lined up my shot, took my practice swing, and then went for it. My club made great contact with the ball, leaving a small patch of grass upturned with the tee. I watched the ball sail over the pond in a perfect arc and set itself down just in front of the hole. It dropped nearly perfectly, and for a moment I thought I might get a hole in one. It was exhilarating. Who would have thought that I could get such a thrill from hitting a ball with a stick? We walked over to the green, and I tapped the ball about a foot to sink it in the hole.

As I've become more and more familiar with the game and the people who play it, I wonder if my new hobby is really so much at odds with some of the things I value most about poetry. It doesn't cost anything to write a poem, and since poems are worth so little monetarily, they are distributed almost freely. They form a kind of linguistic commons. It's not unusual to hear a snippet of poem somewhere else, as a title for a novel, opening a scholarly paper, or at the beginning of someone's wedding. And while I'm not a Scottish shepherd tooling around with my rock after a rabbit hole, I can still imagine, not too delusionally, I think, that my little public course retains some part of the spirit of the original courses.

This morning I played a quick round. Even on a Wednesday morning, the nine-hole course was busy. Just a couple of holes in front of my group, a father was out playing with his two pre-teen sons. Behind us, there was a foursome of men in their seventies who could barely see well enough to keep track of their balls after hitting them. In the back nine, we passed a group of nattily dressed middle-aged women playing at a leisurely pace and rolling their clubs in pull carts. The golf course felt like its own community, and it's one that is often more welcoming than the academic community where I spend most of my time. The guys in the pro shop always recognize me and sometimes greet me by name. It may be because I stick out as one of the few young women playing regularly at the course, because I am always neatly attired in one of my polo shirts, or because I am almost always smiling widely in anticipation of playing— whatever the reason, it's pretty great. ◈

Asbury Park, Just Before Winter

Jeffrey Alfier

Ambling a few yards from my side,
my eight-year old grandson clomps
along the boardwalk to hear the music
his feet pound out on the wooden planks.
In this beach town that's more postcard
than substance, I point out the sights
to show the balance of reclamation
and desertion in sea-battered facades –
a ship carved above an arcade, the ancient
paint of a clown terminally flaking off
a storefront wall, divers in wetsuits
submerging beneath an undulating dark,
and fishermen planting poles in low tide,
their eyes following sea birds that track
the swarming schools of bluefish.

Soon his gaze shifts to those on boardwalk
benches – a woman whose silver hair
flutters in a damp wind, taking forever
to write something on a calendar; a dazed
young man feeding pigeons sullenly,
as if it were an act of contrition, the flock
bustling about his feet like the grayed-out
aftermath of a coastal storm.

And I think, little man — if in the future
you stray along the boardwalk this same time
of year, you'll come to know there are lives
you could glare into till you never laugh again,
and learn that September is a middle-aged
woman lit by light through a stained glass
window, a month written in seashells gathered
in a previous year and re-found in the home
of aging parents, a month converging

in a solitary figure who claims no home
but a seaward bench, covering his ears
and willing his world into somewhere else.

Words for a Night Singer

Jeffrey Alfier

Comfort's an old print dress – pink,
black and pomegranate. Threads
fraying slowly apart still beg her
to keep it around just one more year.

She won't deny she's got a cigarette
going in every ash tray in the house,
but refutes tall tales she's got a man
in every bar her band books a gig in.

Her husband hears ice cubes tinkling
as she idly stirs her gin. He obliges
with hesitant refills. Come nightfall,
spooning will be their slow dance in bed.

Upstairs, an only child waits on nothing
but solitude as he listens to ambient voices
downstairs. He whispers into an oscillating
fan, thinks the sound comes back as music.

one story

Books with Pictures

Rebecca Chace

I've been thinking about books for hard times. A friend's daughter was just killed in a skiing accident. Another friend's husband went to the doctor because he felt exhausted, and was given less than a year to live. The jugular vein of the earth has been cut open in the Gulf, and nobody seems able to cauterize it. The brain has a hard time wrapping itself around these things. You want distraction, but when you're in shock you have no attention span. The friend whose husband was just diagnosed wrote on Facebook: "Can anyone suggest something good to read? All I can handle right now is *Calvin and Hobbes.*"

A comic book seems like a good idea to me under the circumstances. It's a book with pictures, after all, and these are the very first books we held in our hands, puzzling at the shape of the letters and how easily they transformed in the mouths of grown ups into what we wanted most of all: a story. The front piece of *The Animal Family* by Randall Jarrell, with "decorations" by Maurice Sendak reads:

> Say what you like, but such things do
> happen—not often, but they do happen.

It's an invitation and a dare. The pages of this small, nearly square book are thick like an artist's sketchpad, and each chapter is divided by a drawing: a cliff with a cabin on the beach. The sea with moon and clouds. The characters in the book are a hunter, a mermaid, a bear, a lynx and finally a boy. But there are no figures in any of the drawings. They are places to enter, caves to peer into; there is a bow hanging from the branch of a tree for the reader to pick up and try for herself, the arrows are leaning against a log just below. The book was published in 1965, at a time when traditional families were fracturing, and new ways of forming a family were being explored. *The Animal Family* is a love story not only between the Hunter and the Mermaid, but between all of the different creatures that find their way home together. As Jarrell writes, "The hunter and the mermaid were so different from each other that it seemed to them, finally, that they were exactly alike; they lived together and were happy." It is a book that offers not only escape but solace. Each of the characters enters a world they have never known before, and there is an acceptance that much will never be understood.

When the lynx plays too rough the hunter tells him: "Velvet paws! Velvet paws!"

The Mermaid, who is learning the hunter's language asks, "What's velvet?"

"I don't know," the hunter said. "But it's what you say to a cat to get him to keep his claws in. My mother used to say it on the boat." So the hunter said it and the mermaid and the lynx understood it, each in his own way—a little scrap of velvet there between the forest and the sea.

There are times when a book can be your home, a shell that you carry on your back. A book with pictures is even better; you can build a whole landscape with that. You are in some hard places, the waiting room at the hospital or the departure lounge at the airport to name just a few. But if you have the right book you can pitch a tent and build a fire, right there on the shore of disaster. ≈

Dante and Beatrice, 2010
A one-act play

A. S. Maulucci

Characters

Dante

Virgil

Beatrice

Satan

Scene

A barren place, open to the sky. Enter Dante and Virgil, followed by three winged creatures who keep a medium distance—their intentions are uncertain, their appearance and behavior alternate between menacing and benevolent.

Dante: Why have you led me here, Master?

Virgil: Because this is the place where she must appear.

Dante: Why *must*? Is she under some obligation or compunction?

Virgil: Only of her own making. She has promised me she will speak to you today.

Dante: That pleases me immensely. I have long wished to hear her voice again.

Virgil: You shall hear it within the hour, of that I am certain. Hers is a spirit which can be trusted. And more than that, I put my confidence in her love for you. Why else would she have summoned me to be your guide through this dreadful place? And if the truth be told, I was glad to leave Limbo even though it means I am forced to witness the horrors we have seen here.

Dante: Is your existence in Limbo so terrible? You at least have the company of great men and thinkers such as Homer and Socrates.

Virgil: And Plato and Aristotle.

Dante: Yes, the great Aristotle too. Companions such as these must help to pass the time.

Virgil: Indeed they do, and I would delight in their companionship were it not for the fact that we are unable to speak to one another. Each of us is condemned to utter soliloquies . . . Yes, we are fortunate to have been spared physical pain, but it is the eternal boredom that is our particular form of torment.

Dante: Then I do pity you, Master. You deserve so much better.

Virgil: I must be happy to submit to what is willed by God.

[long pause]

Dante: Have you noticed the three winged creatures keeping us under close observation? They have been following us since we departed from the main path.

Virgil: Yes, I have seen them.

Dante: Know you their intent?

Virgil: I do not. Whether of good or evil I cannot say. Let us be wary of them.

[Dante sits down upon a boulder.]

Virgil: Are you weary?

Dante: My legs need to rest. *[a brief pause]* How long must we wait, do you think?

Virgil: *[looking up]* I see the Pleiades on the move. It cannot be very much longer.

Dante: Will those sister stars be accompanying her?

Virgil: I see every reason to believe they will.

Dante: Please tell me again how it was she summoned you, omitting no details.

Virgil: *[smiling paternally]* You are like the puppy that whines and watches for his treat. Very well ... A solitary streak of light penetrated the gloom of Limbo, a soft and delicate ray which seemed to come from some distant star and by slow degrees reached out for me and touched me with a tenderness that melted my heart and then grew almost imperceptibly into an enveloping radiance. Then with a sudden shimmer she appeared and I beheld a form that was both angelic and womanly, both suppliant and divine. Her presence entranced me and spoke to me with a kind of music more beautiful than any poetry, and as it drew me closer—

Dante: *[alarmed]* Ahhh! Behind you ...

Virgil: You needn't tell me. I feel the chill in the air. *[He turns to face Satan squarely]* How dare you leave the confines of Hell? How dare you follow us here?

[Satan wears a black suit and homberg hat. He is grinning.]

Satan: I dare to go wherever I please in my own domain.

Virgil: Are we still in your domain? I thought we had left it behind.

Satan: You are on the border of it.

Virgil: Very well. Tell us what it is you want and then begone.

Satan: *[with a smile]* Only to listen. Nothing more. Human love is such a curious thing and so easily turned to hate. The love that this mortal holds for—

Dante: *[standing abruptly]* Do not speak her name!

Satan: *[smiling again with ironic deference]* ... is the purest love that I have seen in a man's heart.

Dante: And what of it? Your ugly words defile it!

Satan: Nothing, nothing. Just forget I'm here. Go on as before.

Virgil: That is hardly possible. Your presence contaminates the very air we breathe.

Satan: Then why did you enter here if you find this place so repugnant? Why did you bring him? You should have remained on the other side of the Gate, and he should have stayed above ground, on earth.

Virgil: He has come here for the purification of his soul. Heaven has allowed it, Heaven has willed it. It is preordained.

Satan: Ah, the purification of his soul. His soul. *[Pause while he ponders a bit. At the mention of Dante's soul, Satan's features undergo a change as he mulls something over, scheming]* And you, why do you guide him?

Virgil: For his own good, and at the request of a Lady.

Satan: Ah, the lady, yes. We come back to that subject. The one who is shortly to make an entrance, as I heard you say.

Dante: She will not come as long as you are here!

Satan: Yes, no doubt she finds me offensive.

Dante: I beg you, Master, make him leave! I cannot tolerate him.

Virgil: I have no power to do so. And I am sure he has no desire to comply with our wishes by doing us such a great favor.

Satan: Quite right! However, I am willing to make a compromise as it were. I will withdraw at a discreet distance where I cannot be seen but where I will be able to hear what is being said. I want to see this lady for myself, and I want to hear what she has to say.

Virgil: *[after glancing at Dante]* Absolutely out of the question.

Dante: *[curious]* Why do you bother to ask our permission when you could do this without our knowledge?

Virgil: Because he wants to strike a bargain with you and thereby worm his way into your soul.

Satan: *[with a kind of cackle]* Quite right, quite right! I can see that your reputation for cleverness is not exaggerated. You see right through the devil's designs. Nevertheless, you will not get rid of me so easily.

[As Dante and Virgil are exchanging glances of exasperation and dismay, Beatrice appears suddenly in a shimmering of light atop a small hill above the others. The winged creatures vanish. Satan crouches down and cowers and then stands up slowly, regaining his dignity somewhat.]

Dante: She has come!

Satan: *[looking around wildly]* Where? Where is she? I do not see her!

Virgil: Of course not. She is not visible to your eyes.

Virgil: But I want to see her for myself!

[Beatrice raises her hand and Satan is forced to crouch down again, only this time he is unable to rise, and as she waves her hand he is driven out against his will. He slinks away on his hands and knees like a whipped dog. Beatrice then walks slowly to center stage. Virgil is on her left and Dante on her right. She stands with hands clasped before her, very still and dignified.]

Virgil: And so you have come.

Beatrice: I am here for a moment only in order to have a word with this man.

[Virgil nods and lowers his eyes, withdrawing respectfully stage left. Dante stands transfixed, unable to speak. Beatrice seems to draw him to her as if by enchantment, and when Dante has moved close enough she raises her hand to stop him]

Beatrice: Ah, how good it is to see you again . . . If only we could spend a while together and speak of what is in our hearts as we never did on earth, but that can never be.

Dante: *[bewildered and a bit overcome]* Dear one, forgive me for asking, but why did you come to such a place as this?

Beatrice: For our mutual benefit and because I wanted to see and know how much you love me. Yes, I still have some traces of vanity in my soul. When you arrive at the Mount of Purgatory we will have no time alone . . . and I wish to tell you something . . .

Dante: Yes . . . ? Please go on.

Beatrice: *[pausing and looking away]* Oh, it was foolish of me to come. *[another pause as she struggles with her higher nature]* My life on earth was preordained in its brevity, and there was little time for us to find our love's way and to enjoy one another as lovers should.

Dante: It is a source of continual pain . . .

Beatrice: I know, my dearest one, but you must stop loving me.

Dante: I never could, nor would I want to.

Beatrice: You must learn to love another in my place. I have much to teach you of Divine Love . . . When I return to Him, my love will become pure spirit once again . . . *[she takes Dante's hand and presses it to her cheek]* . . . but for now . . . my love for you as a man and yours for me as a woman did not come to full flower on the earth . . . It was not meant to be . . . and we never found our friendship . . .

Dante: My love for you will live on in my heart as long as I draw breath, and in my poetry forever . . .

[They embrace.]

Beatrice: I wish to feel your human love as it might have been on earth . . . but it cannot be. *[she releases him]* Once you have been purified our love will be enfolded into the greater mystery of God's love

Dante: You were nine when I first laid eyes on you, a girl of great gifts with an angelic bearing and a face that reflected heaven . . . and as you grew into a woman you carried that purity within you, and you never lost your radiance . . . You are my greatest love and greatest inspiration.

Beatrice: Did you ever wish to know my love, my woman's love?

Dante: I was so in awe of you . . . I worshipped you . . .

Beatrice: I have no right to ask this now and yet I must. Would you have been happy just to be my friend or did you wish to know my love as a woman?

Dante: *[hesitating just a bit]* What I remember most vividly now is the longing to touch your hair, to kiss those perfect lips, to caress your neck . . . Whenever I saw you my heart became enflamed with a passionate desire to take you in my arms, and that desire would give me no peace. After your death, you became the star that guided me, and your memory taught me to make our love a source of inspiration for my poetry . . . I mourned you for many years but then a profound alteration began to take place as you were transformed in my mind into a great beacon of hope and truth . . . Can you understand this?

Beatrice: This is what I had expected to hear, but yet I hoped for something different, I don't know what . . . perhaps not to be glorified so much . . . *[she takes a step back]* No, no, no, this is only my human weakness returning. It is not right that I should love you now. I must leave you here, but we will meet again once you have left this place and passed through Purgatory.

[Beatrice draws back, turns, walks slowly away, and disappears. Dante remains standing in silence as Virgil re-enters from stage left.]

Virgil: Courage. You will see her again soon. But now we must return to the darkness.

[Virgil leads the way upstage, and Dante follows with head bowed.]

[Satan returns. He addresses the audience.]

Satan: I could not hear them. I heard nothing. And you, you heard every word. Tell me what they said. Tell me what she said. What does she look like? I promise to give you everything you ask for if you will tell me what I want to know. *[Pause]* Speak out! I command you in the name of the Darkness! Speak, or be forever damned!

[Satan stares fixedly and intensely at the audience. A light comes down as if from Heaven. Satan struggles with this beam of light which bears down and crushes him. All the lights fade to black.] ❧

Fugue for a Man and a Woman
a poetic drama

A. S. Maulucci

fugue n. 1: a polyphonic musical composition in which one or two themes are repeated or imitated by successively entering voices and contrapuntally developed in a continuous interweaving of the voice parts 2: a disturbed state of consciousness in which the one affected performs acts of which he appears to be conscious but of which on recovery he has no recollection.

—Webster's Ninth New Collegiate Dictionary

Scene

A bare stage with a man and a woman seated on stools or simple chairs facing away from each other. Imagine them seated at opposite ends of a sofa or sitting up in bed together. The woman is reading a book. Occasionally, they look up at the audience as if appealing to a tribunal. Only at the end of the play do they turn to face one another.

Man: This is my sister—wife—a strong woman . . . dedicated to her own quest for truth . . . She's a woman who loves truth more than she loves me . . .

Woman: I love him . . . really . . .

Man: She *says* she loves me . . . Let that be enough . . .

Woman: He says he loves me, but it's not enough . . . A person has to love truth more than anything . . . A person must exist alone and apart, without reference to anyone, in order to be a pure, independent being with a well-defined identity . . . Once strong alone, a person can be stronger with love . . .

Man: I define myself by loving her . . . But do I love her for herself or for what I want from her? . . . I don't know . . . She's disappointed me so often . . . I'm not really sure I'm capable of loving anyone . . . Then why go on? . . . Is a life without love worth living?

Woman: I've had to work so hard for love as I've had to work for everything else in my life . . . Nothing has been easy for me and everything has had its price . . . Has it all been worth it? . . . Perhaps . . . it's too soon to tell . . . I want to love and be loved absolutely, inconsolably, undyingly . . . I want to be swept away by passion . . . But I cannot force the issue with life . . .

Man: Life is more than an issue . . . or an unanswered question . . . or an unfulfilled quest

Woman: My first love for him has been tempered by experience . . . He must learn to accept that and let me love him in a new way, my own way . . . he must have patience . . . This is a new cycle in my life . . . he must wait for passion to possess me again . . . Until then, he must be satisfied with knowing I loved him once . . . He must learn more about me . . . By knowing me better, he will eventually come to respect the truth that is in me, and his love for me will grow deeper . . .

Man: There must be a foreknowledge of finality with love . . . A sense that it exists absolutely and finally . . . a trust in its uniqueness . . . and a profound certainty that without it one would perish . . . More than anything I want to give myself up to her . . . I want to commit myself body and soul to my love for her . . . I want to love her purely, simply, absolutely . . .

Woman: But without permanence . . .

Man: Nothing in life is permanent . . .

Woman: Not even truth is permanent . . .

Man: She's a cynic . . . incurable . . .

Woman: Inevitable . . . He's such a muddle-headed romantic . . . and he sees me through a rose-colored glass . . .

Man: She's reading again . . . Night after night . . . living beside me but not *with* me . . . with me but not *of* me . . . alone and apart from me . . . I want to shock her out of this self-absorption . . . crush her in an embrace . . . murder her with passion . . . I want to kill the truth in her, the truth that she can live without me . . . And that is the reason I hate her

Woman: I love his hatred . . . It is the proof of his love . . . It makes his love more believable somehow, makes it real and true . . . I could not trust his love for me unless I believed that he hated me too, because I know I am worthy of his hatred . . . But can he ever know the part of me that is totally unconnected to him? . . . Can he love me in that place he is forbidden to enter?

Man: I've tried to understand her . . . her impetuous moods . . . her frenetic energy . . . her self-annihilation and denial . . . her need for truth and her negation of me . . . but there is a part of her that is mysterious and unreachable . . . I am bewildered by the part of her that has no connection with me . . . Sometimes we speak a different language . . . and sometimes we are silent . . . Yet I know that deep down we are the same . . . we have the same needs, the same vulnerabilities . . . How can I ever grasp the totality of this woman if she keeps a huge part of herself locked away from me? . . . How can I give her what she wants if she won't let me understand her needs? . . . How much longer can I go on begging for intimacy without losing my self-respect? . . . I wish she would understand this

Woman: I have no desire to understand him anymore . . . I've given up trying to get inside his head . . . I have lost all my passion for him . . . Maybe I just know him too well, and the mystery is gone . . . He's become predictable . . . He's in a rut, stagnant . . . No growth, no change . . . I don't know why he goes on living . . . I don't know why he stays with me . . . He's not even hateful to me anymore . . . I am indifferent to his existence . . . I have sunk down into a bog of apathy and ennui . . . It matters nothing to me whether he is here or not . . .

Man: I don't know why I stay with her . . . She's shut me out of her life . . . We live in two solitudes . . . She seems so unhappy . . . I want to help her fulfill herself . . . I want her to help me fulfill myself . . . Are we one another's impetus or impediment? . . . Are we helping each other to stand or pushing each other back down? . . . Very hard to say for sure . . . We didn't know very much about who we were when we got married, but we made each other feel more alive and believed it would be that way forever . . . How impulsive and irrational we were . . . I had just tasted success and I wanted a family . . . I felt powerful and alive . . .

Woman: I had my own career when I met him . . . He asked me to give it up so we could have children . . . because *he* wanted a family . . . How stupid and naive I was then . . .

Man: The first year of our marriage was wonderful . . . We were totally caught up in each other and we were the two happiest people on the planet . . .

Woman: In the second year of our marriage I got pregnant, and I loved being pregnant much more than I'd ever thought possible . . . I loved it more than anything else in the world . . . I discovered more love in me than I'd ever known . . . My baby just grew inside me . . . He just grew and grew, as if I'd swallowed a magical seed that an angel left on my pillow . . . He was warm and heavy inside me . . . He was wrapped inside my body like the best Christmas present I could ever imagine . . . but he kicked his way out too soon. Like all men he was impatient to be born . . .

Man: I used to lay my head on her belly and listen to his heartbeat, that miraculous little signal that said, "Let me out of here!" . . . He wanted to join us both . . . He wanted to come into the world and be a part of both of us . . .

Woman: The truth is, I wanted him all to myself . . . Why deny it? . . . I sobbed when he was torn from me . . . He came out too soon . . . He was weak and as sensitive as an open wound . . . Why couldn't he have just stayed inside me forever?

Man: He was born too soon, and he was sickly . . . but I loved him all the more . . . he was still my son even if he wasn't very healthy . . .

Woman: He wanted a normal, healthy baby boy, not the deathly thing that I gave him . . . Was it my fault that he was born too soon?

Man: We had it all, but the boy changed everything . . . She gave up on me when he was born . . . She loved him to exclusion . . . A kind of madness possessed her to have him all to herself . . . She was consumed by her love for him . . . Why couldn't she have shared her love with both of us?

Woman: He became more selfish and self-centered after the baby was born . . . When I was too tired to make love or too busy with the baby he got angry . . . He resented the baby for needing so much of my attention . . . Was it my fault that he was sick all the time? . . . When I was too exhausted to make love or too busy with the baby to cater to his every whim he got angry and stormed out of the house . . . Was it fair to expect my whole life to revolve around him?

Man: I wanted her to show me some affection, to pay some attention to me . . . Is that so unusual? . . . I started feeling like I was some kind of robot that went out to work every day and brought home a paycheck at the end of the week...What is marriage supposed to be about anyway, just raising children?

Woman: A woman cannot love a man who is inconstant, ambivalent, or indecisive...at least I can't, I'm not made that way...I need a man who is sure of himself, sure of what he wants...He blew hot and cold on the subject of a family...One day his world revolved around me and the baby and the next he needed time to himself to sort things out...How long could I be expected to put up with that?..."Make up your mind," I told him, "either you're in this marriage or you're not. You can't be both a husband and father and a free spirit, so which is it going to be?"...He agonized and he struggled, he vacillated back and forth, and life with him became hellish...He was no longer gentle and tender with the baby and me...he stopped caring about our needs...

Man: A man cannot love a woman who doesn't need him...She was so strong, so independent of me...She and the baby would've done fine without me...She didn't need anybody...I admired her for that, but it didn't make it any easier to love her...

Woman: Of course I knew he wouldn't live very long...he was a deathly little thing...and I paid no attention to the doctor's lies...A mother knows...He was so frail...His eyes were so big and full of wonder...He loved to listen to music...He slept deepest when it was raining and I lay beside him...His little finger twitched when he was nursing...but he was a deathly little thing, and he wasn't given much time on this earth...A mother knows...

Man: She started ignoring me...gave all her love to the boy...the two of them were always holding on to each other, sitting together like a madonna and child...He was my son too, wasn't he?

Woman: What can a man know about having a child?...It's the ultimate love...No man can appreciate that...

Man: Was it so unreasonable to expect her to share him with me?...I wanted to be close to him, to love him with a father's love...But she blocked me out as if I didn't exist, as if I'd served my purpose and was no longer needed...

Woman: His death deadened my feelings...I knew I could never love anyone or anything again...

Man: Her heart died with him . . . It was as if she had fallen into a black hole . . . She was lost . . . It was impossible for me to reach her . . . The way she looked at me sometimes was scary, hollowed out, or full of blackness . . . as if I had killed him . . .

Woman: Nothing could touch me anymore . . . Not love . . . Not pain . . . Nothing . . . The moment he died I ceased to exist . . .

Man: When we buried him . . . I saw her eyes . . . and I knew there was no love left in her . . . Now she says I should go away, or if I want to stay, stay, and just let her be, let her live in her own way . . . But I know "her own way" means nothing but a cold, empty heart . . . and growing old together . . . I don't want to grow old without love . . .

Woman: The colder I become, the more he needs me . . . It's perverse, but the more he needs me, the colder I become . . . I know it's cruel, but the more he needs me, the more I despise him . . . How can he live with a dead woman? . . . Why doesn't he just go away and leave me to my . . . self?

Man: "Just live your own life," she says, "and don't worry about me." . . . I would live my own life if I had one without her . . . "Just be yourself," she says, "and maybe I can learn to love you again." . . . I have always avoided the truth about myself . . . who would I be without her? . . . "Just stay where you are," she says, "and maybe one of these days I'll come back to you." . . . I would do anything to reach her but doing nothing is the hardest thing . . . I know I should leave her . . . but where would I go?

Woman: He has lost his way with me . . . He's lost his bearings in life . . . He is not the man he used to be, sure of himself and sure of where he was going . . . a man with the power to bring me to life . . . He is only a bittersweet memory . . . I am in mourning for the passing of what we were, and for the thwarting of what we could have become . . .

Man: She eclipses me when I am with her . . . She used to bring out the best in me and now she just blots me out . . . And yet I still want to be with her . . . Am I crazy? . . . How could I let myself become so dependent on her? . . . She has become the source of everything I love about my life, everything I need, the source of all my pleasure and power, and I am hooked on her like a junkie! . . . I hate what I have become . . . She has turned me into what I am, a sickly, dependent thing, an emotional cripple . . . She has destroyed the man I once was . . . And I hate her for it . . .

Woman: We are like fire and water . . . or a force, and the absence of a force . . . One of us will be destroyed . . . One of us will cease to exist . . . It's inescapable . . . truth must prevail . . .

Man: We are chained together . . . If one of us plunges into the abyss, the other plunges with him . . .

Woman: I must free myself of him . . . I must destroy him if necessary . . . I am the stronger, and I must survive . . . If there is any truth to existence, the stronger must survive . . .

Man: Life is not an issue, a question, or a quest . . . It cannot be reduced to a simple equation of right and wrong . . . The truth and its opposite are incompatible and mutually exclusive . . . but they can both exist . . . Life is big enough for both of them . . .

Woman: Truth is not created or destroyed . . . It is only changed into another form . . .

Man: The truth is that there is only destruction and birth . . . Out of the ashes, the Phoenix rises in triumph over death . . . and a new cycle begins . . .

Woman: Change is the only constant in life . . . I must free myself of him . . .

Man: I must be free of her . . . If one of us plunges, the other plunges with her . . .

Woman: Without him, I can live again . . .

Man: Without her, I can be born again . . .

Woman: He does not complete me . . . He ends me . . .

Man: We are not the completion of each other . . . I will not be incomplete without her . . . We are not two halves of a whole, we are two wholes linked, two circles interlocked at the circumference . . . We are ying and yang fitting snugly together but distinctly separate . . . It will not be impossible to live without her . . .

Woman: It is impossible to live with him . . . It is impossible to live one more day with him . . .

Man: One more day with her will kill me . . . I must be strong . . . I must act decisively, now or never . . . Is she still reading or has she fallen asleep? (Turns to *Woman*.) Darling, are you awake?

Woman: I must have dozed off. (Turning to *Man*. Anxiously.) Please hold me. (They embrace.) You won't ever leave me, will you?

Man: Of course not . . . Don't ever think such a thing . . . I would rather die than leave you . . . ❧

Fugue for a Man and a Woman in performance

Fugue for a Man and a Woman is called a play for voices because the performers do not move around the stage but rather sit in chairs or on stools or stand at lecterns. The simplicity of this concept allows for a great deal of freedom in staging the play—it can be presented as minimalistically or as elaborately as the director would like or the budget permits.

Stage performances have varied considerably, from a bare stage at the Quebec One-act Play Festival in Montreal (1976) to a multi-media production at Three Rivers Community College in Norwich, Connecticut (1997) involving live music and projected images.

The format could also accommodate modern dance interludes embodying some of the complex emotional states suggested by the interweaving monologues—the author likes to think of them as psychological-emotional arabesques—of these separate but interdependent characters.

The author strongly recommends that music be used, with a different instrument representing each character. Some possibilities: a violin for the woman and a cello for the man, or a flute/guitar combination. If a single instrument is preferred, a piano, saxophone, or cello would work best.

Fugue is also especially suitable for the very intimate medium of radio. Music is essential for this type of performance. A radio production broadcast on Connecticut Public Radio in 1981 had music scored for synthesizer and electric piano by Michael Leonhardt with a man's theme/woman's theme that intensified the emotional impact of the play.

It is also quite feasible to perform *Fugue for a Man and a Woman* as a chamber piece in a bookstore or classroom. The author and his wife read it at The Reader's Feast Bookstore in Hartford, Connecticut (1991) as part of the author's poetry reading. In a conference, or workshop setting, participants can be seated around a table or in a circle of chairs. The script can be read by two individuals or passed around a "reader's circle" with everyone reading. Participants may want to explore some of the issues raised by the play, or a workshop leader may wish to use the script as a catalyst for discussion in couples or family therapy.

An earlier version of this play was published in Connecticut Artists Magazine, Winter 1980-81.

Fugue for a Man and a Woman Performance History

La Biblioteca of San Miguel de Allende, Guanajuato, Mexico, with BC May and Phoebe Greyson, 2010.

Three Rivers Community College, Norwich, Connecticut, with students Bill Wolcott and Allison Desrosiers, 1997.

The Reader's Feast Bookstore, Hartford, Connecticut, with Anthony Maulucci and Jan Tormay, 1991.

Connecticut Public Radio, with David Keith and Frances McDormand of the Yale Drama School; musical score by Michael Leonhardt; directed by Faith Middleton, 1981.

Quebec One-act Play Festival, Montreal, Quebec, with Anthony Maulucci and Elizabeth Mudry of the Montreal Theatre Lab, 1976.

An Inheritance

Dan Pope

One afternoon I found a call on the answering machine from my Aunt Helen, asking for bread. "I want Vermont Bread," she said, "raisin cinnamon, please." There was a second message adding orange juice to the list, no pulp. A third asked me to leave the groceries on her doorstep, because she was feeling ill and she wouldn't want me to catch her cold, just ring the doorbell and she would slip the twenty dollars—

The machine cut her off.

I got dressed and drove to the store to get what she wanted. It took me a while to find the bread among the gourmet foods at nearly four dollars a loaf. When I rang her doorbell, nothing happened. I banged on the door with my fist. "I brought the food," I announced. She was eighty-nine and all but deaf. I banged away for a couple of minutes. I was out ten bucks and didn't want to go away empty-handed.

So I turned the handle and the door opened.

"Aunt Helen," I called. "It's Ronnie. I've got your bread here."

She lived alone in a two-story Colonial, the smallest house on the street. I went up the creaky wooden stairs and looked into the two bedrooms. The place was filthy, piled high with all sorts of bag-lady crap—newspapers, grocery bags, a depressing assortment of tin cans and plastic trays. I went down to the living room and den, checked the bathroom.

I found her on the floor in the kitchen.

Two weeks earlier I had returned to my father's house in Wintonbury, Connecticut, where I had grown up. He had flown south for the winter and I was taking care of the place until spring. He usually just drained the pipes, locked the doors, and had a neighbor look in from time to time, but that winter I needed a place to stay.

I'd had a job in New Jersey for the past sixteen months, working for a community college. I lived in the basement of a defunct fraternity house on the edge of campus and took my meals in the student cafeteria. It was a sweet deal. The college took a few hundred bucks from my pay every month for taxes, insurance, and housing, and the rest went directly into my bank account. I was in the maintenance department. When I say maintenance, I don't mean pushing a broom. It was electrical work, roofing, carpentry—whatever came up. I could do all that stuff, since I was board-certified. My father was a general contractor, and he'd had me working jobs since I was fourteen. "You know a trade," he always said, "and you'll never go hungry." His advice was dead-on. I'd had seven years of undergraduate education and nearly enough credits earned for a BA in

Philosophy but I'd never managed to procure a paying position based on those qualifications.

I liked New Jersey because you could go into a bar and light up and blow smoke all over the room. You didn't have to stand outside and shiver like a vagrant. No one likes to rush a cigarette. The point is to wind down: beer, barstool, cigarette. The three went together. The coeds were a distraction, the way they marched around campus, smelling like heaven. When did girls start to look like that? Dress like that? It must be something in the milk, the wheat, the water, the cell phone signals, the high-def heat, the wi-fi frequencies. The end of the world was near, but the girls did not know it and they had never been comelier, all costumed, as they were in North Jersey, like strippers on holiday.

One night a pack of them barged into my preferred drinking establishment, a dive called Sully's, situated at the entrance to an industrial park. I was coming up on my fortieth birthday. Maybe that partly explains my actions. Two of the girls came back with me to my basement room for some beer pong and I got a little out of hand with the paddle. I'd thought them a wee bit older. I did not learn their ages—eighteen and eighteen, respectively—until the campus police arrived and informed me of this fact. Alas, there was a non-fraternization clause in my contract.

In short, I got terminated without severance pay.

The emergency room doctor told me that Aunt Helen had pneumonia. It was good that I brought her in when I did, he said, because she was severely dehydrated and malnourished. They admitted her and I went home, out ten bucks for the groceries.

That winter, I mostly just hung around the house with the furnace roaring away, watching the snow fall. I stayed up until four or five in the morning. Name a movie that played cable that year and I can tell you the plot. In the afternoons I went into town and sat in the coffee shop, reading the print off the newspaper and observing the daily routines of the harried housewives. (Is there any creature in nature as nervous as the suburban housewife? Chihuahua? French poodle?) That was my occupation, watching housewives and high school girls and making pithy observations to myself (see above) and snarling whenever some jackass in a business suit came too close to me with his cellphone in operation. With approximately six hundred and fifty dollars left over from the New Jersey job and a rent-free abode, I had no need or desire for employment.

A week later the hospital called and said they were ready to discharge Aunt Helen.

"Okay," I said.

The woman asked me about my care plan.

I said, "Yeah, well, she gets along pretty well by herself. I bring her groceries once in a while. She's a feisty old broad."

"With whom am I speaking, please?"

"Huh?"

"What is your relationship to the patient?"

"The nephew, you can write down."

"You are aware, sir, that your aunt is demented?"

"Demented?"

"That's correct."

I was watching TV and wasn't paying much attention to the conversation. "As in raging lunatic? That sort of demented?"

"Excuse me?"

"You should just send her home in a taxi," I suggested. "That would be the easiest thing to do."

"Hold, please."

A few minutes later a doctor came on the line. He explained that my aunt needed twenty-four hour supervision at a residential facility. Since she lacked capacity, I would have to sign for her as conservator or guardian. Under state law, they couldn't release her without a plan in place.

"Actually, I'm not her primary care-giver," I explained. I thought the phrase sounded correct in the circumstances. "My father is. I can have him call you, if that's convenient."

"You understand that she cannot remain here. This is a hospital, not a nursing home. Technically she's already been discharged. We no longer have a bed for her."

"Where is she?"

"At present, in a wheelchair in the emergency room waiting area."

"Okay, then. I'll get back to you with that information."

I hung up.

I called Florida to inform my father of these developments. His answering machine—a relic from the late eighties—had no greeting, it just gave one long beep and then the line went dead. Was the cassette filled? Broken? I called for two days without getting an answer. In New Smynra, where he lived in a condo on the sixteenth floor of a concrete tower built on sand, you could drive up and down the main drag all afternoon and not see a single snowbird. They were there, thousands of them, holed up in their apartments and condominiums, but they only came out for dinner, like pelicans diving into the sea the hour before sundown. There was a shuffleboard court in town, but my father didn't engage in that sort of silliness. Mainly, he liked watching TV, like me.

Meanwhile, the hospital called ten times a day, speaking to the answering machine. "Mr. Milton, would you please come to the hospital to make arrangements—." I didn't answer those calls. I would look at the caller ID and let the nurses talk themselves blue. I didn't need that sort of aggravation. Aunt Helen herself called once too, from a payphone in the lobby, I presume, leaving the following message:

"Salvy? Salvy? Come get me, Salvy. I'm in the hallway with terrible people."

Salvatore was my father's name.

Finally, one afternoon, my father's Florida number appeared on the caller ID.

"Dad, where the hell have you been?"

"Nowhere. Why?"

"You got your hearing aid turned on? I've been trying to get a hold of you since Monday."

"Maybe the ringer doesn't work."

I filled him in on the medical developments, just as the doctor had explained them to me—the diagnosis, the requirements of state law, etc.

When I finished, he said, "Go get her. Take her home."

"Didn't I just explain it to you? They won't let her out—"

"Sign whatever they want. Just get her out of there."

"You better call them."

"What the hell can I do from down here?"

"Besides, she's a lot better off if they keep her, you know? I mean, she's demented. That house, have you seen that place lately? She's got shit piled to the ceiling. It's a fucking catastrophe—"

"She doesn't need any goddamned nursing home. She's no more demented than you or I."

"I'm not so sure about that last part."

"Listen," he said. "Listen to me now. There's some things you don't know."

"What do you mean?"

"I don't want to go into it over the phone."

"What, you think it's bugged?"

"Don't be a wise guy. Just do what I tell you."

"If you must know, it's a royal pain in the ass. She doesn't even remember my name any more. And I'm out ten bucks—"

"Son, listen carefully. Are you listening?"

"Yeah."

"She can't go into a nursing home or those bastards will take every cent she's got. Her house, her savings, everything."

"What savings?"

"That's the part I haven't told you."

Once upon a time, Dad had had four older sisters, all of them spinsters. About ten years ago they retired and moved into that matchbox Colonial. Their house was a half-mile away from his, on the other side of the town's public golf course—to the right of the seventh green, to be precise. My father often found soggy Titelists in their backyard. He would collect them and bring them home and put them in a five-gallon glass jug on his hallway table, all these grass-stained and bruised golf balls jumbled in the glass, like a modern sculpture.

For the past decade, he'd checked on the sisters every day, sometime two or three times a day, performing the same sort of maintenance I'd been doing in New Jersey, and tasks of a more menial nature as well—filling their car with gas, taking out the damned garbage, bringing them groceries every Sunday afternoon. It had practically been his full-time job since he'd retired from the contracting business, and he'd grumbled about it plenty. The only break from duty was when he flew down to Florida for a couple of months every winter, and the aunts would get along with assistance from church volunteers and Dial-a-Ride. I knew all about that. I'd helped out too, when I was a kid, cutting their lawn, but mostly I avoided them. I had no desire to get sucked into that septuagenarian chasm. They had always been old, it seemed to me, these four unpleasant women with moles blossoming on their faces and necks, wearing the same moth-eaten, wine-stained sweaters, dining on white bread and canned sardines. The four left the house only for Sunday Mass, as far as I could tell. And none of them believed in doctors; they just rotted away when they got ill. One by one the aunties had dropped into the netherland, leaving Aunt Helen the last standing spinster, the hardiest of the lot.

What I didn't know, and what he now disclosed, was this:

Aunt Helen was loaded.

The four spinsters had worked compulsively throughout their miserly, barren lives (occupations: schoolmarm, librarian, secretary, town clerk), stuffing their paychecks into the bank every Friday afternoon, and once retired, they did the same with their pension and Social Security stipends. All of this currency had been bequeathed to Aunt Helen and burgeoned under my father's wily stewardship. In ten years, he'd more than doubled the holdings with some timely buying and selling of his favorite stock, the warmongering United Technologies.

"How much?" I asked.

"Including the house? A half-mill."

"Seriously?"

"More or less."

"You son of a bitch. A fucking half-million. Why didn't you tell me?"

In truth, I couldn't blame him. I'd gone through a healthy share of Dad's assets in my forty years, a good deal more than the typical son or daughter was entitled—the possessions I'd whisked away in the night, the costs of rehab and attorney fees, not to mention the aggravation I'd caused. I wouldn't tell me about a family fortune either. But my wild years were behind me now, I figured, despite my recent mishap in New Jersey.

"It's not something I intended to keep from you—"

"It's okay, Dad. I understand."

"Son, that money's meant for you and your brother. I don't need it. It was going to go to you all along. You hear me?"

"Yes."

"So you're in charge now. It's up to you. Don't let those vultures get a dime."

"I'm on it, Dad."

"Good boy. Oh, one more thing."

"Yeah."

"What year did Columbus sail the ocean blue?"

"Is that a joke?"

"It's her ATM code. Find the card. Get the money out while you can." He hung up.

A half-million dollars, I thought. I felt my chest expanding with an emotion suspiciously like the onset of love.

I had an assignment. There would be no more HBO marathons. My brother wouldn't be any help. He was off in the far east—in a Buddhist monastery in Thailand, the last we'd heard. I didn't tell a soul. None of my friends in town could be trusted with a half-ounce stash, let alone a half-million bucks. I shaved for the first time in a long while, got into a suit, and headed downtown.

At the hospital, the social worker took me into her office. Patients suffering from dementia tend to wander, she told me. "We don't know why, but they feel compelled to walk. That's why she needs a secure facility." I listened intently, scratching my chin. She laid out pamphlets and price lists. The least expensive place wanted twenty grand up front.

"What about home release?" I asked.

"We don't recommend at-home care for this type of patient."

"Hypothetically."

"Well, it would have to be round-the-clock supervision by certified professionals. And, by state law, we would have to inform the D-E-S."

"D-E-S?"

"The Department of Elderly Services. There would be unannounced visits by a state agent to ensure an appropriate environment and proper patient supervision."

"We want the best for Aunt Helen."

"Of course you do."

It took some time, but I convinced her to release Aunt Helen into my care. I signed at least six forms, assuming full and total responsibility for her welfare. I didn't read the papers, I just kept scribbling my name.

The social worker gave me a list of businesses that provided home healthcare services. "I recommend a battery of certified nursing professionals, working in eight- or twelve-hour shifts," she said.

"That's exactly what I had in mind," I said.

She led me into the emergency room, where Aunt Helen was sitting in the hallway in a wheelchair, a blanket over her legs. In her lap she held her handbag. I said hello, but she appeared wholly catatonic. It wasn't a good day for Auntie. She peered at me with intense concentration, a look which I recognized from old photographs, when she was a plain and unhappy young schoolteacher. Perhaps she'd been near-sighted and had never been diagnosed. Or perhaps that baleful squint was simply her natural expression, the one she'd used at Robert F. O'Brien Elementary School since 1946, terrifying generations of third-graders so severely that her visage would appear in their dreams for decades after they'd finished all manner of schooling.

The social worker and a security guard helped me wheel the patient out to the parking lot and load her into my piece-of-crap Honda. She was wearing the same clothes she'd had on when I found her on the kitchen floor, beige slacks and a blood-stained gray sweater. Her right eyeball was bruised, where she'd landed.

I strapped her in and gunned out of the parking lot. I lowered the window on her side, to suction away the aroma. She clearly hadn't bathed that day, or maybe not at all during her hospital stay.

About halfway to her house, as we crossed into Wintonbury, she perked up: "Where are you taking me?"

"We're going home, Aunt Helen. Isn't that exciting?"

"Put the window up."

"Fresh air is good for you. It'll clear all the bad hospital germs out of your lungs."

"I'm cold."

I have to admit I was overjoyed with myself. I wheeled into her driveway and shuffled her into the house, holding my breath. I found the groceries—the Vermont bread and orange juice—on the floor in the plastic bag where I'd dropped them ten days ago. I'd forgotten to lock the door, but no one had bothered to break in.

"Here we are," I said. "Safe and sound."

She sniffed and looked around. Her expression clarified. "Will they come for me?"

"Of course not. You're all better now." I handed over the plastic bag. "There's the bread you wanted. That should tide you over."

"Oh, my raisin cinnamon." She had a fearsome grip on her handbag, clutching it like a fullback on a one-yard plunge.

"Let me hang up your handbag for you, Aunt Helen."

"You've done enough already. I know how busy you are."

"It's no problem at all. I'll put it right here for you." I opened the closet door and pointed at the hook on the back of the door.

She sniffed. "Could you turn up the temperature?"

"Certainly."

I checked the thermostat in the living room. It was at 81 degrees. The radiators were clanking and humming. Aunt Helen liked a warm house. Even in summertime, my father told me, she would crank the dial into the nineties, all that oil burning night and day. I turned it down ten degrees.

"All set," I said.

"You're a good boy, Ronnie."

She seemed her coherent self, ensconced in those happy surroundings, so I decided to get on my way. There was no rush.

"If you need anything, call me."

"What?"

You practically had to scream to get her to hear you, she was so deaf. Although, oddly, at times, she could detect a whisper from across the room. I yelled my goodbyes and closed the front door behind me.

Next morning at 9:15, the phone woke me. Anyone who knew me knew not to call at that hour. I picked up the receiver and mumbled, "What the hell?" The caller identified herself as Mrs. So-and-So from the Department of Elderly Services. Unaccustomed as I was to using my faculties at these hours, it took me a few moments to understand that this was not a wrong number and that I shouldn't tell her to go fuck herself.

"What can I do for you?" I said.

"You can open the door," she answered curtly. "I've been ringing the bell for five minutes."

"Oh," I said. "You're at my aunt's house?"

"I am."

"Wait right there."

I jumped out of bed, dressed, slicked down my unruly hair, loaded a few tomato cans into a shopping bag and raced to Aunt Helen's house, nearly skidding out of control at the turn around the 14th green.

A small white car was parked in her driveway. As soon as I got out of my piece-of-crap Honda, a lady emerged from the car, holding a clipboard. She was a middle-aged gal wearing a pinched expression, with tiny shoulders and enormous, rolling hips, like a lady in a fun-house mirror.

"I stepped out to do the shopping," I said, waving my plastic bag.

"I see," she answered in a troll's voice.

I opened the door, calling, "Aunt Helen, I'm back with the groceries."

The television was blaring in the den, a human voice as loud as a fighter jet. From the doorway the D-E-S lady and I peered into the room. Aunt Helen was sitting on the couch, nibbling a piece of raisin cinnamon toast. On the TV, a nun in a brown habit sat behind a desk, pontificating at ungodly volume. The Catholic Channel, her favorite. My father said she watched Mother Angelica night and day.

I stepped into the room and turned down the volume.

"Aunt Helen, there's a nice lady here to see you."

The D-E-S woman lowered herself into a chair across from Aunt Helen and leaned forward to address her, ballpoint and clipboard at the ready. The room smelled vaguely of urine.

"How nice of you to come," said Aunt Helen. She finished her piece of toast and folded her hands in her lap. She seemed to think the lady was from the church. "Have you seen Father Alphonso? He has a wonderful singing voice, but sometimes I think he's awfully young."

The D-E-S lady proffered a litany of questions: How old are you? What year is it, could you please tell me? Where did you sleep last night?

In response, Aunt Helen sniffed four or five times, and her right eyeball seemed to bulge.

"Well?" the D-E-S lady prompted. "Can you at least tell me your name?"

Aunt Helen said, "Get out of my house. Get out before I call the police."

Then she turned back toward the TV, picked up the remote and cranked Mother Angelica to ear-damaging decibels.

After this interview, the DES lady patrolled from room to room, jotting. A pigsty, that house, with all that bag-lady crap piled everywhere. There were old newspapers and magazines and hymnals, glass bottles and tin cans filled with pens and pencils, needles and tweezers, brown shopping bags by the thousands, a plastic tub filled with buttons. Behind all this whatnot, the walls and ceilings were dust-bunnied and spider-webbed, the rugs unvacuumed apparently since placement, the refrigerator infested with fungi, the shelves empty but for a moldy head of lettuce and frozen chicken bones. The linoleum was streaked with a brown substance which may have been mud but probably was not, that had been stepped on and dragged about.

Each time Mrs. So-and-So made a notation on her clipboard, I winced.

Outside, standing by her car, she peeled off a pink sheet, the bottom copy, and passed it to me—the list of violations. She'd checked nearly every box. Underneath she'd scrawled: *No evidence of supervision what-soever—*.

"You have forty-eight hours to rectify the situation," she said. "I strongly suggest that you retain full-time assistance. I'll be back to see that you do."

Back at my father's house, I went immediately to sleep. I had always been a big believer in the restorative powers of the nap. And, as usual, I woke refreshed and clear-headed, a plan of action already formed in my mind.

I went into town and read the newspaper at the coffee shop. For dinner I had a slice of pizza at the parlor next door. Then I came back home to watch TV for many hours. When the grandfather clock chimed midnight, I went into the kitchen and lifted the key off the hook next to the wall phone. My father had hung it there before leaving for Florida, despite my protestations that I didn't want any part of it. *Just in case*, he'd said.

The golf course was silent at that hour, a snow beginning to fall. I parked at the end of the driveway. The place was as dark as a grave, not a single light visible inside or outside the house. I turned the key in the lock.

Inside, the heat was blasting. I turned on the hall light and checked the thermostat. She'd cranked it to 95 degrees. I opened the door to the hall closet and looked inside. I crept into the living room and checked the couches and chairs, looked beneath the cushions, peered inside the cabinets and bookshelves. Next I searched the kitchen. I even looked inside the refrigerator-freezer, because old ladies will keep their valuables in the craziest places.

When I returned to the hallway, a voice called out, giving me a fright:

"Salvy? Is that you?"

"Yes."

"Would you like a glass of warm milk?"

"No, thank you."

"I hear noises."

"That's me."

"Should I call the police?"

"Nope."

"Where are you?"

"I'm checking the furnace. Go back to sleep."

I opened the basement door and went down to the cellar—finding another fearsome trove of bag-lady treasure piled against the walls. The oil burner thundered away, the fire hissing inside the steel chamber, and through the casement window I could see a sliver of the night sky and the snow falling onto her backyard.

Finally, I went back to the first floor and looked into the den.

She was sitting on the couch, clutching her purse, the TV hissing with white noise.

"You're not Salvy," she said.

"It's me, Ronnie," I said. I stepped into the light coming from the television set. "See? It's your nephew."

She picked up the phone. For a moment, I considered pulling the plug out of the wall, but I didn't need to go that far. She knew exactly one telephone number, my father's, the only seven digits that remained in her gnarled and short-circuited cerebral cortex. This was the magic number, the number that made things appear and disappear. *Salvy, there's some papers here from the bank. Salvy, something's wrong with the oven. Salvy, we need milk.* For years my father had been fielding those calls, fulfilling her requests. Now she said into the receiver:

"Salvy, there's people in the house."

While she was preoccupied, I bent and gently tugged on her hand-bag. She didn't resist. It slid out of her hands and into mine, an old black-vinyl thing, torn around the edges. I fished around in her purse until I found it—her ATM card. Then I passed the handbag back to her and she accepted it and clutched it again.

I said, "Do you want me to help you upstairs? I could fix the bed for you, if you like."

"No."

"Wouldn't you be more comfortable in your own bedroom?"

"I met Lucky Luciano once," she said.

"Is that so?" In truth, I'd heard the story scores of times. She'd tell it at every family gathering, practically verbatim from one recitation to the next.

"It was in Naples," she said, "in 1953. He called to me from across the square. I don't usually speak to a gentleman without a proper introduction, but in his case I made an exception. The man had black eyes, the blackest eyes you've ever seen."

"I'm leaving now, Aunt Helen."

She didn't take her gaze off the hissing television screen. "He asked me to marry him, just like that. We hadn't spoken more than ten words. I declined, of course, but I often wonder if this was the right decision. One only gets so many offers in a lifetime. What do you think?"

I said, "I'll lock the door behind me."

I emerged into that snow-covered night and raced to the bank.

What year did Columbus sail the ocean blue?

I punched in the code and there was a momentary lull—and then the dumb machine came to life. Is there a better sound than the shuffling of those twenty-dollar bills before they emerge from the slot? It was like the opening of a door onto a spring morning. The sound of freedom. Five hundred dollars was the daily limit, but there were so many days to come. ❧

I Probably Let Some of It Slip Once

Jonathan Starke

Let me tell you what I'm afraid of.

I'm afraid I will leave you, Laura. See myself behaving too much like my mother each day, hiding Jack Daniels in empty soda cans and falling down drunk on the porch steps, calling, *help me, sweetness, help me. I've fallen.* Then one day I will look at your soft olive face and realize I don't love you anymore. I never really loved you. But you look so much like her—my mother—that height and skin tone and posture and small body.

I'm afraid of never sleeping again. The Sandman has not visited in so many years, has not thrown his brown dust in my eyes, has not hit me over the head with his sleeping stick. Sometimes you are there when the broken sleep comes, the awful nightmares—bullets ripping through my chest, my body tied down and my jaw forced to chew on glass, my brother and father dropping me from the high point of the inside of a cathedral, and I fall and twist to the cross-painted floor. It drives me to such sickening lengths that my dreamself will not blink while bashing a man's head onto concrete, closing off a windpipe with a tight hand, raping a woman who has done nothing but walk past. My realself, me, I wouldn't do those things. I couldn't.

I'm afraid I will abandon our children. If they do not look enough like me. If they do not act enough like me. What if they are mostly made of you? If they carry no gene for passion in their little bodies—for boxing or tangents or samurais or kite strings. There might be a time I hold them like I held a tiny kitten once, so delicate and un-talking and squirmy. Will I wonder what such a small thing would do if thrown from one end of the room to another, even if it is made up of my own parts, even if it is myself I am throwing then?

I'm afraid of the large bugs in the walls. Have you seen them? The ones that rush around the bathroom, come out through the dark holes looking to feed. They see me—*freeze*—hundreds of legs stopped and suctioning against the cold paint. So much worry when I flip on the lights (Will they be there? Could enough of them consume me?) that smashing them with a scrubbing brush, scraping them from the wall, watching their legs drip from the bristles to the toilet, is both marvelous and awful. Something about it reminds me of when I cry in the shower and have to cover my mouth so you will not hear me.

I'm afraid the things my brother predicted about me have come true. He said we were like the two brothers on the TV show, *Wings*. Joe and Brian Hackett. He would be Joe, the successful and straight-laced one: admired, respected, well-off. I would be Brian, the shameful and disastrous one: begging for money, sleeping around, no idea how to settle, love, keep my feet and hands from moving so much. I have asked my father for money. I have asked my brother for money. I have never come to terms with satisfaction or what good enough really means. Always this moving. Always this running. It has hurt you. I know this.

I'm afraid my strength is all gone now, both inside and out. The body-builder I once was, crushed to granite rubble, the gray dust flying up and away—*poof*. Do you love me still with this frail body? How could you, can you, with what you had before? The other me. With a mind that was growing and chewing on knowledge, swallowing it down in an information digestion that held. That stuck. And now you tell me you are leaving me for your parents' place. I can't remember the day, the time, when it is you will be going to them. Where did my muscles, smarts, and memories go? How? How did they leave me like such a fast blowing wind?

I'm afraid my father will die. It is something I have thought about since I was a child, since our mother left us when I was two. Did I ever tell you about the eulogy? I spoke one for my father when I was ten. I did this out loud in the shower. I cried and beat my fists against the tiles. How could I understand that he is so giving, so soft, so strong, but I feel like I have never truly known him? Will never know him. Have you ever seen a manatee? That is my father, only he roams the land. That is how I see him. You probably know some of this. I probably let some of it slip once.

I'm afraid of the truth. To tell it. To hear it. You ask me why I can't just be normal like everyone else, why my compass points in all of these strange directions at different times and places. I have never been able to answer that for you. All I have done is try to philosophize, to point it out to you with one of those slim, metal hands. I tell you it isn't something that can be easily said or shown. We are who we are, what we've become now, and there really is no way to walk backward over the snow tracks, brush the fuzzy flakes so they cover the previous tread. I try and explain this, even as you shake your head and tell me everything I say, am saying, is bullshit. And always has been. ❧

NOX by Anne Carson

Amy Scheibe

My mother says to me, "I bought that book you've been tweeting about, but I don't know how to read it. Should I take it out of the box it came in first?" I tell her that would be a perfect place to start. I can hear she's intimidated, knowing that the book is considered "poetry" but also having read someplace that it's heavy on translation of some long ago dead Latin poet named Gaius Valerius Catullus. Then she says, "Your aunt bought a copy too, based on your status update on Facebook. Not sure if she'll get it either, but we'll try." I say, "That should do the trick."

My seven-year-old son, Bo, walks through the house, the thick gray box that contains *Nox* balanced on one hand, a small Matchbox car sitting precariously on top of the skinny strip of photo that shows Anne Carson's brother, Michael, as a boy of about seven. In Bo's other hand is a toy airplane. He seems to be in the middle of incorporating *Nox* into the labyrinth that is the upstairs playroom—or from his view, the airport. He's been constructing one airport on the floor out of a number of diverse objects all summer, as well as turning an entire wall in his room into a white board and drawing an enormous, O'Hare-worthy terminal in blues and reds. I tell him to give me the book. I need it to do my job, I tell him. He looks at it, says "Who's that?" I say, "My friend's brother." He says "Did he die?" And I say, "Yes, he did, now please give it to me." He hands it over, disappointed.

About a year before Bo was born, or maybe the year itself, I came into brief possession of a small cloth-bound book pasted with a photo strip of a boy wearing swim goggles and dressed in a swim suit and sporting swim fins in the middle of a grassy lawn. The object burned in my hands—I knew it had been in the making, that it was coming to me for a visit, and that it would eventually have to go elsewhere. The brevity of that moment expands now that, all these years later, I have in my hands a perfectly rendered facsimile. Even though I've read it before, my feelings of trepidation echo my mother's—but mine are rooted in knowing that I *will* understand what's in here, not that I *won't*.

A bitch of the first order. This is what Gordon Lish said to me sixteen years ago as he handed me the stack of pages that would become *Plainwater*, Anne's first collection with Knopf. I was an editorial assistant, Gordon was leaving Knopf to "seek other opportunities," and all of the authors on his list were snapped up by other hungry editors. Based on his paltry recommendation, no one wanted Anne. Sonny Mehta changed my life, assigning me—at two months into the job—one of the finest poets alive. Like the wife of an abusive spouse, Anne was first reclusive, shy, not wanting to speak on the phone, but instead only by letter. Eventually I learned that Gordon yelled at her when he would call. They would get into epic battles of obstinacy over his method of editing entire poems out of the book with a giant red X and no other notes. Eventually she refused to speak to him. He had wooed her—or so it went—away from New Directions, probably in some literary land grab that only Gordon understood. Faced with Anne's placid refusal to accept his sweeping edicts, he promptly decided he had made a mistake, and held to that belief firmly. I ran into him at a Barnes and Noble five years later and the first and only words out of his mouth to me were "are you still publishing that no-talent Anne Carson?" By then I had edited a few more of her books, she had won a MacArthur Grant, and well, I don't think I need to say who the bitch of the first order really was.

At some point during those years I remember Anne telling me about her brother, and how he had completely disappeared when she was in her twenties. I also remember her telling me that he had reappeared shortly after her mother had died (waiting in vain for just one more letter from him) and how his response to the news had been "Yes, I guess she is." The well of Anne's voice as she repeated his words was full of a child-like awe, as though she had been looking up at him for so long she couldn't find down. Then not long after, she called me and slipped into a conversation about copyediting that she was planning a trip to see her brother, but he had died instead.

When *Nox* first appeared in that brittle, hand-crafted, and daunting edition I was destroyed by its combination of brevity and beauty. For whatever reason Knopf couldn't publish it—I'm not even sure I still worked there then. I do know that the slim elegy went on a few journeys before landing safely back in the arms of New Directions. Now, restrained by the coffin-design of its grey-flannel box, *Nox* accordions out, fold after fold delivering tiny pin-pricks to the solar plexus, razor nicks to the heart. Where Anne had carefully taped pieces of evidence, or stapled sliced ribs of blank negative film, there is now a necessary flattening of reproduction—but no flattening whatsoever of the raw meat of emotion that is Anne's true gift.

I could certainly wax rhapsodic about how brilliant this book is, or give you my take on why she deconstructs the framing poem word by Latin word throughout, but really who cares what I think of Anne's gracefully fumbling attempt to capture the pain of losing a brother she never really had? Instead I will tell you what I'm planning to tell my mother now that I've finished its reincarnation myself. Read it. One word at a time. It will take you where it wants you to go, and unfold in so many deft and mysterious ways that you will not have time to think about how you got there. Just read it. ∾

Index

The following is a listing in alphabetical order by author's last name of works published in *Post Road*. An asterisk indicates subject rather than contributor.